Jira Mastery for Scrum Masters

Your Complete Handbook for Agile Project Excellence

Dr. Francis Mbunya

Radah Education

DEDICATION

This book is dedicated to all scrum masters who are ready to do what it takes to master skills needed to become a scrum master of value.

Table of Contents

Chapter 1
Introduction to Jira

About Jira

Jira is a popular work management tool used by software development teams to plan, track, and release software. It is highly customizable and can be used to support a variety of agile methodologies, including Scrum, Kanban, and hybrid approaches.

Here are some other key points to consider:

- Jira can be used by teams of all sizes and from a variety of industries.

- Jira offers a variety of products and deployment options.

- Jira templates and solutions can be used to get started quickly.

Benefits of using Jira

Atlassian's Jira stands at the forefront of project management and issue tracking solutions, providing our software development teams with a robust platform for efficient collaboration and streamlined workflows. The benefits of utilising Jira within our software development processes include:

- **Enhanced Collaboration:** Jira promotes seamless collaboration among cross-functional teams, allowing for real-time communication and coordination.

- **Agile Project Management:** Tailored for Agile methodologies, Jira supports iterative development, sprint planning, and continuous delivery, empowering our teams to respond swiftly to changing requirements.

- **Customization for Diverse Projects**: Jira's versatility enables customization of workflows, fields, and boards, ensuring adaptability to the unique needs of our various software development projects.

- **Visibility and Reporting:** Gain transparency into project progress with Jira's reporting and dashboard features, providing valuable insights for data-driven decision-making.

Overview of Jira editions

Jira is available in four editions:

- **Jira Software:** This edition is designed for software development teams and supports agile workflows such as Scrum and Kanban. It also includes features for tracking bugs, managing releases, and reporting on progress.

  - Key Features: Agile workflows, bug tracking, release management, reporting

- **Jira Core:** This edition is a more general-purpose issue tracking tool that can be used by any team to track work and collaborate on projects. It includes all of the features of Jira Software, but excludes the agile-specific features.

  - Key Features: Issue tracking, collaboration, reporting

- **Jira Service Management:** This edition is designed for IT service management teams and includes features for managing customer requests, tracking incidents, and reporting on service performance.

  - Key Features: Customer request management, incident tracking, service performance reporting

- **Jira Work Management**: This edition is designed for business teams across marketing, operations, sales, HR, finance, legal, and design. It includes features for managing tasks, tracking projects, and collaborating on workflows.
  - Key Features: Task management, project tracking, workflow collaboration

Here are some examples of how different teams can use Jira:

- **Software development teams:** Jira Software can be used to track bugs, manage releases, and collaborate on agile development projects.

- **IT service management teams:** Jira Service Management can be used to manage customer requests, track incidents, and report on service performance.

- **Marketing teams:** Jira Work Management can be used to manage marketing campaigns, track content creation, and collaborate on go-to-market strategies.

- **Sales teams**: Jira Work Management can be used to track leads, manage the sales pipeline, and collaborate on closing deals.

- **HR teams:** Jira Work Management can be used to manage recruiting, onboarding, and performance reviews.

- **Finance teams:** Jira Work Management can be used to manage budgets, track expenses, and report on financial performance.

Accessing Jira

To access Jira, you will need a Jira account. You can request an account from your Jira administrator or create one yourself if your Jira instance is configured for self-signup.

Once you have an account, you can access Jira by going to the Jira login page in your web browser and entering your username and password.

If you are using Jira Cloud, the Jira login page is located at:

https://[your-jira-instance-name].atlassian.com

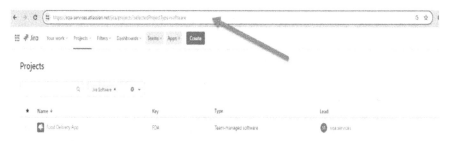

If you are using Jira Server or Data Center, the Jira login page is located at:

http://[your-jira-server-url]/jira

After logging in, you'll be redirected to the Startup page, where you can view all assigned projects and recently performed activities within the platform.

User Roles and Permissions

Jira user roles and permissions control what users can do in Jira. Users are assigned to roles, and roles are assigned to permissions.

There are three default user roles in Jira:

- **Administrator**. Admins can do most things, like update settings and add other admins to the project. They can manage features, customise issue types, and add rules on the board.

- **Member**. Members are a part of the team. They can create issues, edit them, comment on them, move them into different statuses, and generally collaborate on your project's work.

- **Viewer**. Viewers can search through and view issues in your project.

How to assign Project Role and Permissions

In order to assign the role and permission at the project level, Navigate to the project and then the project settings.

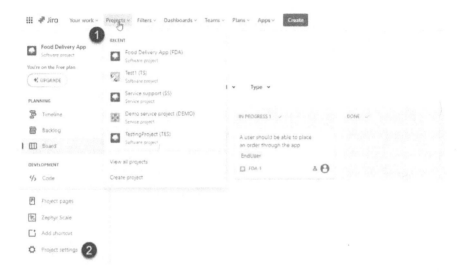

On the project settings, go to the Access page.

On the access page, select the user to which you want to assign/modify the permission and then from the Role drop down, change the role. You have to choose from the Administrator, Member or Viewer role.

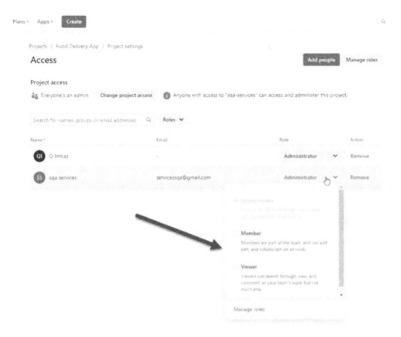

The role will be assigned to the selected user.

How to add custom roles and assign it to the user

Go to the Project> Project Settings> Access and click on the Manage Roles button.

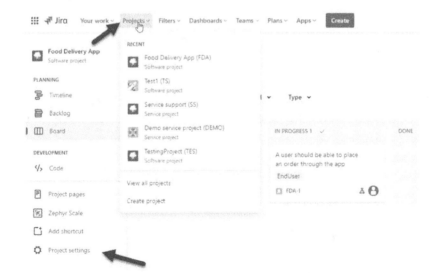

On the manage role pop-up, click on Create role button.

Manage roles

Administrator

Admins can do most things, like update settings and add other admins.

Member

Members are part of the team, and can add, edit, and collaborate on all work.

Viewer

Viewers can search through, view, and comment on your team's work, but not much else.

Create role   Close

On the Create role pop-up, Enter the role name, select the permission of actions that you want to assign to the specific user and click Create.

You can also add users to this user directly from this pop-up or after creating this role.

Create role

Name *

Custom Role - 1

Description *

This is the customized role for external stakeholders

People in this role can:

☐ Administer "Food Delivery App"
   Edit access, manage people and permissions, configure issue types and their
   fields, enable project features, and delete the project.

☐ Manage "Food Delivery App" issues
   Modify reporters and watchers, edit and delete any comments and
   attachments, adjust work log entries, and delete "Food Delivery App"
   issues.   ⌃

   ☐ Add or remove issue watchers
      Add or remove people from the list of watchers on any "Food
      Delivery App" issue.

   ☐ Delete any attachment
      Delete the attachments added by anyone on any "Food Delivery
      App" issue.

   ☐ Delete any comment
      Delete the comments added by anyone on any "Food Delivery App"

Assign this role to:

Name, email or group

e.g. Maria, maria@company.com   🔍

[Create]   Discard

Personalising Your Dashboard

A dashboard is like a personal webpage in Jira where you can put the info you care about. In Jira, users can make their own dashboards and control what shows up on them.

In order to navigate to the dashboard, go to the project and then click on Dashboard.

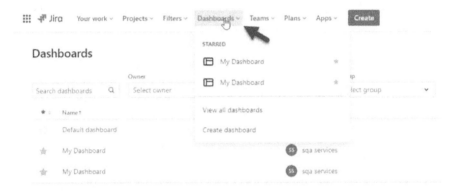

In this option, You will see all the dashboard that are created and you can open any specific dashboard.

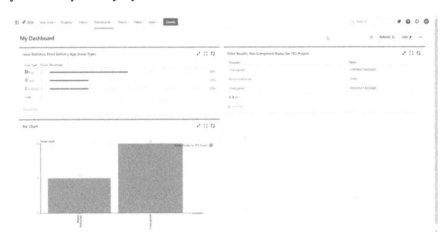

How to create a new custom dashboard?

In the dashboards menu, click on Create dashboard.

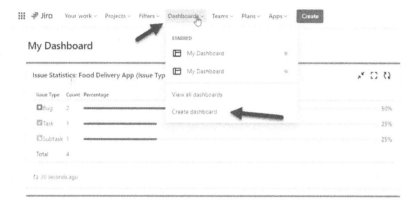

On the Create dashboard pop up, Enter the dashboard name and the description, select the users who can view or edit the dashboard.

You can select from the specific users, groups, any user added on your site, all users on project or select private if you do not want anyone to access and view your dashboard.

Once you have added and selected all the information, click on the Save button.

Keyboard Shortcuts

To enable and view the keyboard shortcuts, press "?" on your jira screen and the pop up will open, from where you can enable and view all the shortcuts.

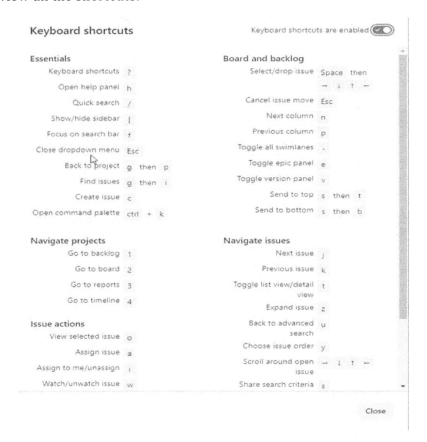

Understanding Jira's Role in Agile Project Management

Jira plays a crucial role in Agile project management. It helps teams organise and track their work in a flexible and collaborative way. Here are some key points about Jira in Agile:

- **Task Management**: Jira helps break down work into smaller tasks or user stories, making it easier for teams to plan and execute work in iterations (sprints).

- **Visibility and Transparency**: It provides a clear view of the project progress through boards, allowing everyone to see what's being worked on and its status.

- **Collaboration**: Teams can collaborate effectively by assigning tasks, commenting on issues, and sharing updates, keeping everyone aligned and informed.

- **Adaptability**: Jira's flexibility allows teams to adapt to changes during the project by easily modifying priorities or adding new tasks as needed.

- **Reporting and Metrics**: It offers various reports and metrics, such as burndown charts or velocity reports, to track performance and make data-driven decisions.

- **Customization**: Jira can be customised to fit different Agile methodologies, enabling teams to tailor workflows and processes according to their specific needs.

In essence, Jira serves as a centralised hub where Agile teams can plan, track, and collaborate on their work, ultimately facilitating efficient project management and delivery.

Chapter 2
Creating and Managing Projects

Jira Software helps your team organise their work better so they can focus on making great software instead of dealing with problems.

A project in Jira is like a folder holding all the tasks (like stories, bugs, and tasks) related to building something. It represents the work your team is doing in Jira Software.

There are different ways to manage work in Jira: Scrum, Kanban, and Bug tracking.

- Scrum works in cycles, good for teams making products regularly.

- Kanban suits continuous work without overloading the team.

- Bug tracking helps follow new features and bugs.

For new agile teams, team-managed Scrum and Kanban projects are simple and easy to set up. These projects grow in complexity as needed. Anyone can make them, but only administrators can make company-managed projects.

Note: If you want to set up a new project in Jira Software, you usually need to be a Jira administrator. Some tasks, like creating a project or changing workflows, can only be done by administrators.

Creating Projects

Log in to your Jira account and select Jira Software from the homepage.

You will be redirected to the Projects page. On this page you can view all your existing projects, and you can create a new project as well.

To create a new project, Click on the Create Project button.

Once you click on the Create Project button, You will be shown a list of Project Templates that Jira supports. You can view a variety of project categories and templates to select from, for example, Software development, service management, Marketing, Operations etc.

We will consider the category of software development, and we get three templates to follow when creating a software development project in Jira i.e Scrum, Kanban or Bug Tracking.

You can select the most suitable template for your project. Let's consider the Scrum template for now. In order to select the template, click on the template name and the section.

Once you select the template, You will be redirected to the main page of the template where you can read about the project type and how Jira allows you to manage it.

To continue, click on the Use template button.

Note:The "Use template" button is available at the top and bottom of the page, you can click at any of it to continue.

Now select the project type you are working on. You get two options to select from that are; Team managed or Company managed. Select the one which is most suitable for your project needs.

For now, we will consider a Team managed project and we will click on the Select a team managed project button.

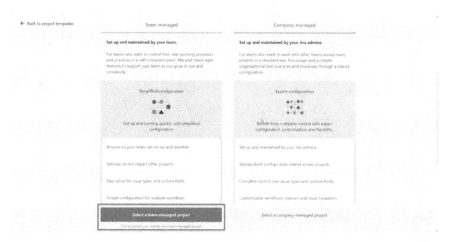

On the next step, name your project and select the access level of the project. Once you name your project, the project key will be typed in by Jira automatically. This project key is the prefix of all your jira tickets. You can change it as well, as per your needs.

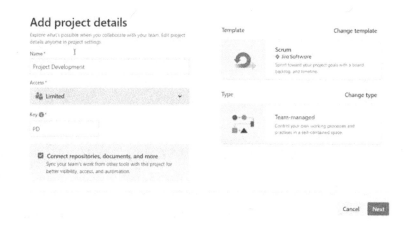

Once you are done, click on the Next button and Jira will create your project.

Before you are redirected to your project, You will be asked to connect some tools, you may skip it, if you do not need this right now.

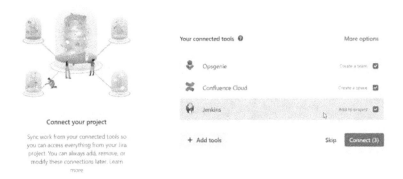

You have now successfully created your first project in Jira. Bravo!

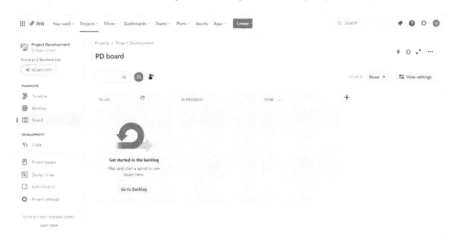

Project Components (Issues, Workflows, Sprints, Boards)

When you have successfully created your project, you can then get started with setting up your project by adding the issue, configuring the workflows (if needed), creating and starting sprints and managing the board as well. We will have a look at all of them one by one.

Issues

To create the issues, You can click on the Create button at the top header navigation bar, or just press the "c" key from your keyboard.

A pop up will be opened, and you will be asked to add the details of your issue.

On the pop-up of Create issue, you will need to add the following information;

1. Issue Type (Story, Bug, Task, Epic) - Required

2. Summary/Title - Required

19

3. Description

4. Status

5. Assignee

6. Labels

7. Sprint

8. Story point estimate

9. Reporter (by default it will be your user) - Required

10. Attachment

11. Linked Issues

Once you have all the required and optional data, click on the create button at the bottom of the pop up to successfully create an issue.

You can also go back at any time and make the required changes in the issue that you created earlier. The most common occurrences when a normal user updates an issue is to change the status of the issue to Progress or Done, changing the assignee or post a comment on the issue regarding any discussion or share the progress on it.

Backlog

Backlog in jira is a collection of all the issues that needs to be completed in order to complete and deliver the project. You can access the backlog of the project by navigating to the left menu, and click on Backlog under the Planning section.

Once you add any issue in your project, It can be shown here in the Backlog list.

Sprints

A Sprint in Jira and Scrum is a time-bound period during which a team works on a set of tasks to achieve specific goals.Sprints are usually one, two, or four weeks long. At the end of the sprint, a team will typically have built and implemented a working product increment.

Creating a Sprint

Navigate to the Backlog screen, and click on the Create Sprint button.

A new sprint will be added with increment in the number.

Starting a Sprint

In order to start the sprint in Jira, Go to the backlog screen, and first move the tasks from the backlog to the sprint. You can do this by dragging the issue from the backlog section to the sprint section or open the issue and then assign the sprint number in the

Sprint field.

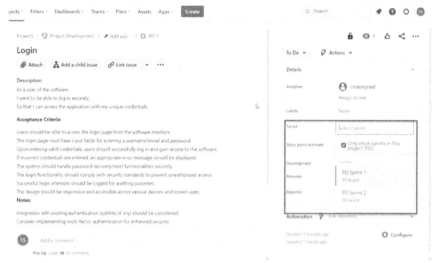

Note: You can not start the sprint, until you have not moved the issues to the sprint.

Once you have moved the issues to the sprint, click on the Add dates option and then add the start and end date, sprint goal and click on the Update button.

Once the dates are updated, You would then see that the Start Sprint button has been enabled on the backlog screen. Clicking on the Start sprint button will kick in your sprint in Jira.

You can create multiple sprints in your backlog if you want to plan further ahead. Also, you can add more issues/tasks into your ongoing sprint, if the team has the capacity.

Completing the sprint

When all the issues of the current sprint have been completed and marked as Done in Jira, you can then mark the Sprint as complete in the Jira.

In order to do that, Navigate to the Board page from the left menu, and on the Board, you would see the Complete Sprint button.

Click on the Complete Sprint button, and Jira will mark the sprint as completed.

Please note that, if your sprint has some tasks which are not marked as completed in Jira, then it will ask you to move the incomplete issues to the next sprint.

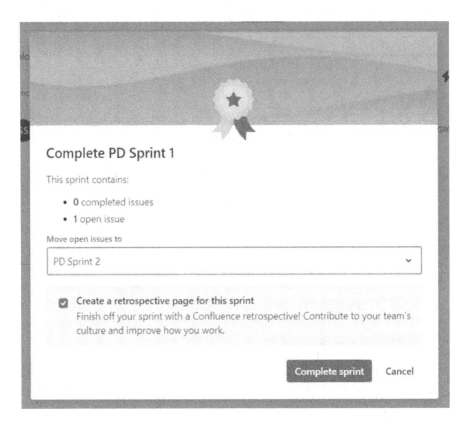

Complete PD Sprint 1

This sprint contains:

- 0 completed issues
- 1 open issue

Move open issues to

PD Sprint 2 ⌄

☑ **Create a retrospective page for this sprint**
Finish off your sprint with a Confluence retrospective! Contribute to your team's culture and improve how you work.

Complete sprint   Cancel

Jira Board

A board in Jira shows your team's tasks as cards you can move around. These cards represent tasks, called "issues. The board usually mirrors how your team works, showing where tasks are in your team's process.

There are three default columns on your team's board:

1. "To do" - where new tasks start.

2. "In progress" - where tasks are actively being worked on.

3. "Done" - where completed tasks end up.

These columns help your team track and manage the progress of work as it moves through different stages.

In order to navigate to the Board, click on the Board from the left menu and you will be able to see the progress of your project on the Board for the current sprint.

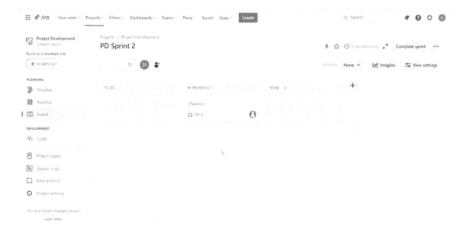

You can move the tasks from your board as well, or if you want to add some more issue types, you can do that as well.

Manage Workflow

Each project in Jira includes tasks called issues, which your team can access, modify, and progress through different stages. The route these tasks follow is known as a workflow. A Jira workflow comprises statuses and transitions that guide an issue from inception to conclusion. It typically mirrors the work procedures within your company.

In order to view or modify the existing workflow on your Jira Project, Navigate to the Board screen and click on the three dots at the right corner of your screen. Once you click on it, go to

Manage Workflow.

This button will redirect you to the workflow screen. Here you can view your current workflow set up for tickets.

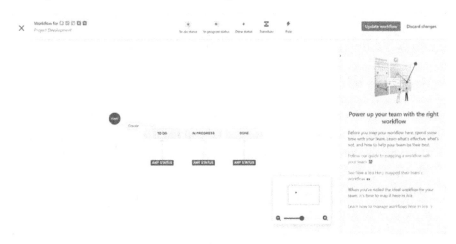

You can modify the workflow by making the required changes in the workflow editor. For example, By default Jira allows you to change the issue status to any status, but, if you want to have a restricted rule like a user can not directly move the To Do issue to the Done status. Then you can create a transition that every To Do issue must go to In Progress first and then Done. You may refer to the screenshot below, which shows a capture of the modified

28

workflow.

Once you have completed the changes, click on the Update Workflow and users would not be able to move the To Do issues now directly to Done.

Configuring Project Settings

Project settings in Jira allows you to change the project settings, name, access level and much more related to the specific project. In order to navigate to the Project settings page, Go to your project and click on the Project settings from the left menu bar.

You will be redirected to the Project settings page and you can view different levels of project settings that you can change.

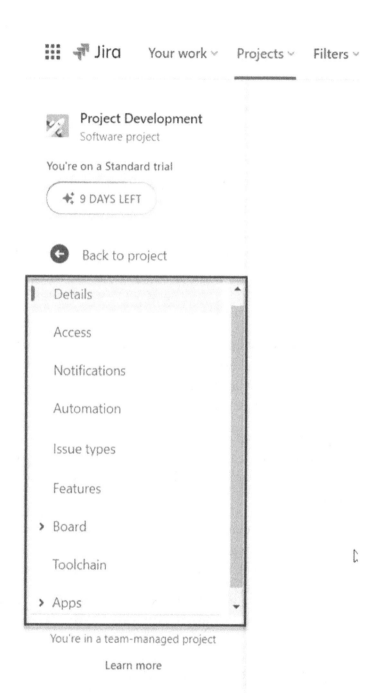

Let's take an overview that what configuration that you can do at project level;

- **Details**: You can change the project name, project key, project lead or the default assignee of any issues that you create on the project.

- **Access**: Change the access level of the project, change the role of any user or add any new people to your team.

- **Notifications**: Select on what events you want Jira to send you a notification on email or on Jira.

- **Automation**: Streamline and automate various processes, tasks, and workflows within the JIRA platform. It allows users to create rules, known as automation rules or automation triggers, to automate repetitive actions, notifications, assignments, and other routine tasks without manual intervention.

- **Issue Types**: By default, Jira provides some standard issue types such as task, story or a bug. In case you or your team is in need to add a new issue type in a project, you can add it from here. Such as improvement issue type etc.

- **Features**: You can enable or disable some features of Jira on your project as per your requirements. For example, You can enable or disable the releases, deployments and reports from here.

- **Board**: You can configure or customise your Jira board from here. From adding some more columns to your board to making some custom filters, you can all do it from here.

- **Toolchain**: Discover integrations for your tools, connect work to your project, and manage it all right here

- **Apps**: Jira allows you to install third party apps or add ons to boost your productivity and enable you to do more. You can manage your third-party apps from here.

Project Permissions

There are two types of permissions in Jira, one is for company managed projects and another one is for team managed projects.

Permissions schemes for Company-managed projects

- Jira administrators manage project permissions for company-managed projects through permission schemes.

To manage the permission for the company managed projects, Click on the settings icon at the top header beside your profile

Click on Issues

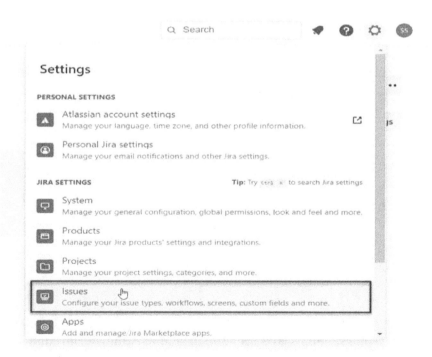

Select the Permission schemes for the left menu

You will have all your permission schemes mentioned here. Permission schemes are created to manage the permission at a project level.

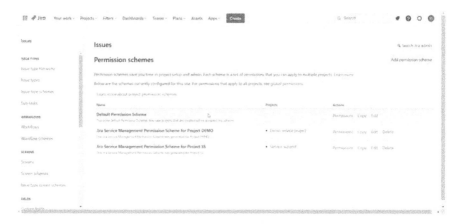

Since we are working on a default permission scheme for any project in Jira and not for a service related project, We will click and go to the Default Permission Scheme's permission action.

Under the permissions, you can view and manage all the permissions and grant it to any group of users, specific user, Public, Project lead and many more.

Permission roles for team-managed projects

- Project administrators manage project permissions for team-managed projects through custom roles

In order to create and manage role, You can refer here : Jira SOP - Chapter 1

Cloning and Archiving Projects

Cloning the project

When you want to clone/copy a complete project without any manual intervention, currently the only possibility is through third-party apps; however with a few manual steps, you can achieve similar results with regards to the cloning of a project.

The cloning can also be done by import/export capabilities available within the jira.

Archiving the project

As a Jira admin, archiving inactive projects is possible, including their issues, components, attachments, and versions. Archiving doesn't impact shared schemes, workflows, issue types, or content among other projects.

Archived projects' issues won't display in basic or advanced searches. While direct access to these issues remains, editing them is restricted.

In order to Archive any project, Navigate to projects > View all projects

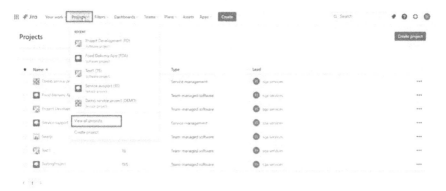

Select the project that you want to archive, and then click on the Archive option under the list.

Jira User Interface and Navigation

In Jira, you can move around different screens to finish your work. But not every task needs you to go through many screens. With the new navigation system, you can do more tasks without having to switch between screens as much.

Sidebar

The majority of users perform their tasks within the project setting, be it on the board, queue, or issue view. Introducing menu items to the sidebar of the project brings your app closer to where users actively work. You can go to your project timeline, board, backlog and project settings from here.

You can also add your favourite apps or shortcuts to the sidebar menu for the quick access purposes.

Top bar menu

Jira Cloud's main navigation bar gives you quick access to the projects, filters, and dashboards you use most. It also lets you create issues, search and access help notifications and Jira settings.

From the top bar menu, You can navigate to different projects, filters, apps or dashboard. Also you can search the issue or go to your profile settings.

Tip: The quickest way to get to a recent board from anywhere in Jira is by clicking the search field (or pressing / on your keyboard). You'll see recent boards, projects, and filters in the bottom half of the search panel

Chapter 3
Entering Work in Jira using Issues

Understanding Jira Issues as Work

Issues are like the foundation of a Jira project. They could be a story, a bug, a task, or something else in your project.

Jira is used by various groups to follow various types of issues. These could range from a software glitch to a project job or a request for time off. In Jira Software, issues help you handle code, estimate how much work is needed, and stay updated on your team's progress.

Issue keys are made up of two parts:

1. The project key (SMART in the screenshot below)

2. A unique and sequential number (Auto assigned to every issue you create)

Note: To set up and make various kinds of issues beyond what Jira provides by default, you'll require an administrator role.

Issue Types (Epics, Stories, Bugs, Tasks)

Issue types distinguish different types of work in unique ways, and help you identify, categorise, and report on your team's work across your Jira site. They can help your team build more structure into your working process.

Let's explore now the different types of issue types in Jira Software;

Epic

A big user story that needs to be broken down. Epics group together bugs, stories, and tasks to show the progress of a larger initiative. In agile development, epics usually represent a significant deliverable, such as a new feature or experience in the software your team develops.

In order to create an epic issue in your software project, Open your project in Jira and click on the Create button.

Once the pop up opens, Select the issue type as Epic and enter your epic's details.

Create issue

Required fields are marked with an asterisk *

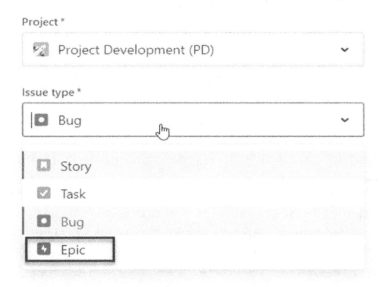

Once you are done with the details, click on Create

You have now successfully created an Epic.

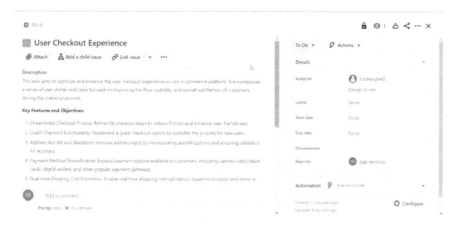

Best Practices to create and maintain epics in Jira:

- Clear and Concise Description: Ensure the epic description is comprehensive, providing a clear understanding of its purpose.

- Regular Updates: Maintain regular updates to the epic to reflect the current status and any changes.

- Granularity: Break down epics into smaller, manageable user stories for better implementation and tracking.

Story

A user story is the smallest unit of work that needs to be done.Similarly, to create a story in Jira, Click on Create button and when the pop up is opened, select the issue type as Story.

Create issue

Required fields are marked with an asterisk *

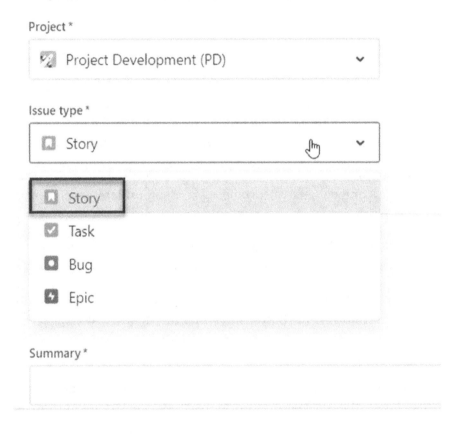

Project *

🖼 Project Development (PD)   ⌄

Issue type *

📄 Story   🖑   ⌄

📄 Story

☑ Task

⬛ Bug

⚡ Epic

Summary *

☐ Create another issue

Add in all your details like story description, status, assignee etc, and then click on Create button.

Your user story will be created.

Best Practices to create and maintain user stories in Jira:

- Clear and Specific Descriptions: Ensure user stories are articulated clearly, focusing on end-user needs and desired outcomes.

- Collaboration and Communication: Encourage collaboration between teams, stakeholders, and developers to refine and clarify user stories as needed.

- Granularity and Manageability: Break down larger requirements into smaller, manageable user stories for effective implementation and tracking.

Task

You can use the task issue type to categorise miscellaneous tasks – like technical investigations, administrative work, or other project-adjacent tasks. To create a task, select the issue type as a task, add the task details and click on Create.

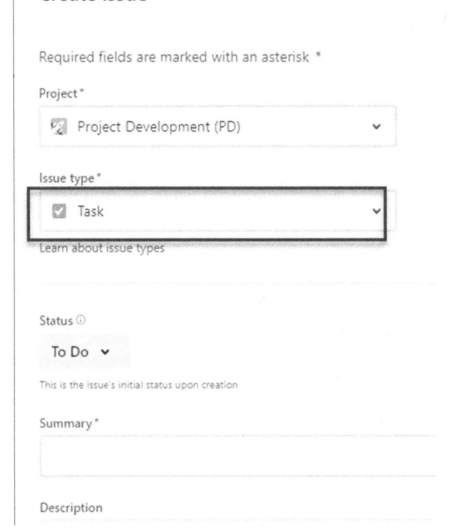

This will create a task in your Jira project.

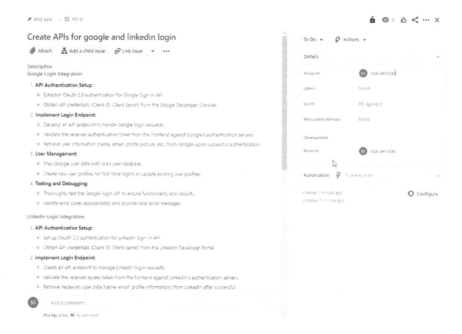

Best practices to add a task in Jira:

- **Clear and Actionable Titles:** Use descriptive titles that clearly indicate the task's purpose and what needs to be done.

- **Regular Updates and Communication:** Ensure consistent updates on task progress and collaborate with team members to address any blockers or changes.

- **Subtask Utilisation:** Leverage subtasks to break down complex tasks into smaller, manageable units for better tracking and execution

Bug

Teams that work in an agile way use the "bug" type to keep track of software problems like mistakes in how things look on the screen, things that don't work properly, or other small issues that users face.

To create a bug, select the Bug issue type while creating an issue in Jira

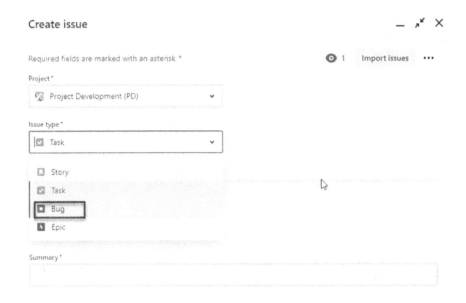

All the details of your bug, like the description, expected results, actual results, steps to reproduce, add any proof (image or videos) and link it with the task/story in Jira in which you are experiencing a bug.

After that, click on the Create button, and a bug will be created,

You can see in the above screenshot, that it has all the details of the bug, also it has been assigned to the person and also linked to the story in which the bug is being experienced.

Best practices to create and maintain Bug issue types in Jira

- Clear and Detailed Bug Descriptions:

  o Create Specific Titles: Ensure bug titles are concise yet descriptive, summarising the issue for easy identification.

  o Detailed Description: Provide a comprehensive description of the bug, including steps to reproduce, expected behaviour, actual behaviour observed, impacted functionalities, and environment details. This helps developers understand and tackle the issue effectively.

- Proper Categorization and Prioritization:

- Use Correct Labels and Components: Assign accurate labels or components to categorise bugs by module, feature, or severity. This aids in organising and filtering bugs, making it easier to address similar issues together.

- Prioritise Based on Impact: Assess the severity and impact of bugs on users, system functionality, or revenue. Prioritise fixing critical or high-impact bugs that significantly affect user experience or system stability.

- Regular Updates and Collaboration:

  - Update Bug Status and Progress: Keep bug statuses updated (e.g., To Do, In Progress, Done) to reflect the current stage of resolution. Regularly communicate changes, progress, or any challenges faced during bug resolution.

  - Collaborate Across Teams: Encourage collaboration between developers, QA testers, and stakeholders by utilising comments, attachments, or @mentions in Jira. This fosters effective communication, idea-sharing, and problem-solving for quicker bug resolution.

Issue Statuses

Issue statuses represent where an issue stands within the project's workflow. By default, projects come with predefined statuses based on templates. These statuses serve as initial recommendations but can be modified or deleted to match your team's workflow. Additionally, you have the option to create new statuses to tailor the workflow according to your team's requirements.

Here's a list of the some common and by default statuses in any project in Jira:

- Open

    The issue is open and ready for the assignee to start work on it.

- In Progress

    This issue is being actively worked on at the moment by the assignee.

- Done

    Work has finished on the issue.

    To Do

- The issue has been reported and is waiting for the team to take action.

Issue Priorities

Issue priorities show how important an issue is in comparison to others. The default priorities include "Highest," "High," "Medium," "Low," and "Lowest." These priorities and their meanings can be adjusted by your administrator to fit your organization's needs. For further details on setting priorities and their explanations, explore the configuration options available.

Here are the default priorities and their meanings:

- Highest: This issue will significantly hinder progress.

- High: A serious issue that might cause progress to stall.

- Medium: Could potentially affect progress.

- Low: A minor issue that can be easily managed or worked around.

- Lowest: A trivial issue with minimal or no impact on progress.

Assigning and Editing Issues

Assigning Issues

After you have created issues and work tasks in your Jira project, and added all the details, the next step is to assign it to your team or the people. In order to do that, open the issue in jira and navigate to the Assignee field on the issue screen

Click on the assignee field and a drop down will populate, in the drop down, you will be able to see a list of the team members that are working under the project. You can then select the person from the list to assign the issue.

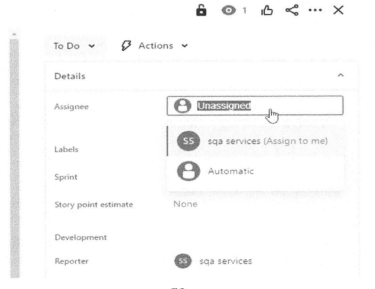

The issue will then be assigned to the person, they will get notified in Jira and over the email as well. Also the issue will be showing on their Jira board and the project's board as well with the user Initials.

Editing issues

Once the issue has been created and assigned in Jira, they are often updated as well, the common scenarios when any one needs to edit/update issue is;

1. To edit the title.

2. To change the assignee.

3. To share an update in the comment, in the comments section. The update can be to share progress on the ticket, share any technical challenge that an assignee is facing.

4. To change the issue type, for example, changing a bug issue type to a sub task.

5. To link it with any related issue.

6. To assign a different sprint.

To edit an issue, open an issue, and change the field you want. For example, if you want to change the assignee, click on the assignee drop down, and change the value.

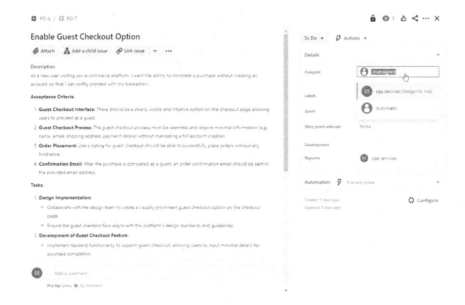

Filtering Issues and Saving Filters

Jira filters help you save your searches, making it easy to redo them without typing the search again. Jira is our project tool that helps find, organise, and handle tasks and projects well. Filters are important because they make work smoother, help us work better, and understand how projects are going.

Creating filter

To search an issue and to create a filter for any specific search criteria, navigate to the search bar at the top of the page and click on it, a pop up will be opened and then click on the View all issue at the bottom of that pop up.

You will be then redirected to the advanced search screen, as shown in the below screenshot.

Now, either you can go basic or be advanced in creating a search criteria. For the basic, click on "Switch to basic" and then you will be allowed to create a search criteria by selecting the values from the drop down.

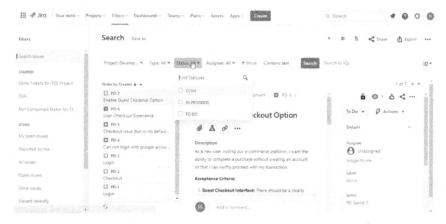

Or, you can click on Switch to JQL, to enter the specific query to search the issue.

Once you have created the search criteria, Jira allows you to save that specific search criteria and that is known as a Filter in Jira terminology.

To create a filter, click on Save as on the same screen, once you have created the search criteria.

Once you click on it, you will be asked to name the filter, enter any name that you want. It would be better if you name it as per what this filter does for example "Issues reported by client". Then click on the submit.

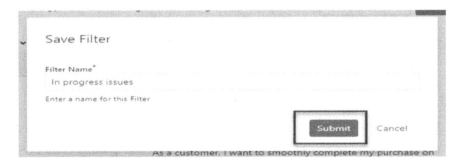

And your filter be saved and shown in the list of all filters.

Viewing and navigating to the filters

On your project, at the top bar, you will see the menu item for Filters, click on it and then click on View all filters.

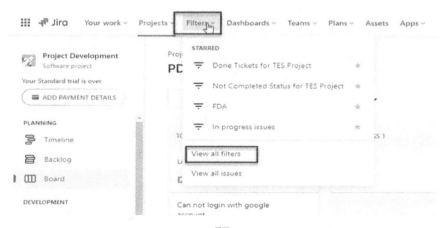

On the filters page, you will have all your created filters. And if you click on any filter, it will redirect you to that specific filter and issue results.

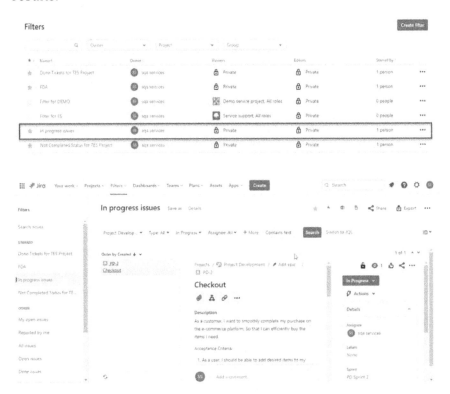

Editing the filter

In case you want to update or edit the filter, open that particular filter, make any changes you want, and click on the save button.

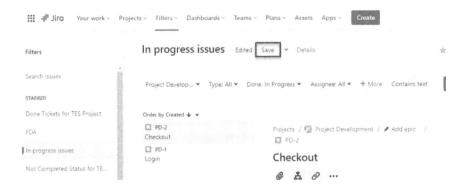

It will save the updates to the filter.

Sharing the filter

You can also share the created filter with any group, team member, project or organisation. To manage that, navigate to all filter screen and click on the three dots, as shown in the screenshot below;

Click on the Edit button.

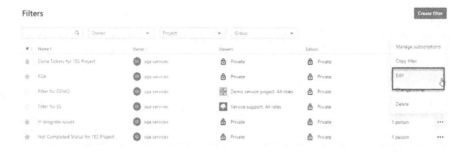

Now you can see that there are two sections; Viewers and Editors. And you see a drop down in each section.

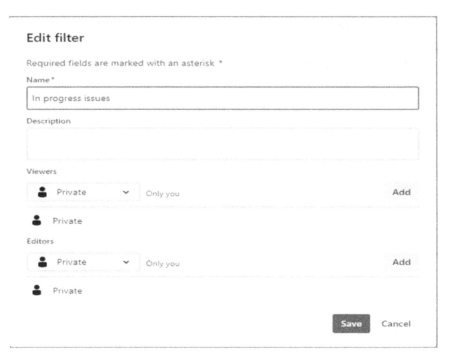

For example, if you want to share this filter with the project team or any individual member, click on the drop down, and select the relevant option.

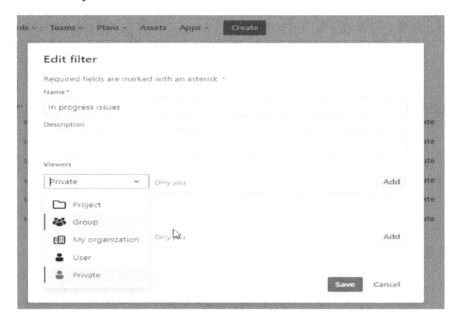

Select the correspondence value, in my case I have selected to share this filter with a project team, so I will select the project name, role,and then click on the Add button.

Once you are done, click on save. The filter settings will be saved and the filter can be accessible by the team now.

Linking Issues and Tracking Dependencies

Linking Issues

Issue linking is a way to connect two problems or tasks in Jira. It helps show how one issue is related to another. For example, it can show if one problem is similar to another, if one task needs to happen before another, or if one task is like a duplicate of another.

Issue linking also allows you to:

- Create a new linked issue from an existing issue in a service desk or business project.

- Create an association between an issue and a Confluence page.

- Link an issue to any other web page.

To link a issue in Jira, Open any existing issue and click on Link Issue

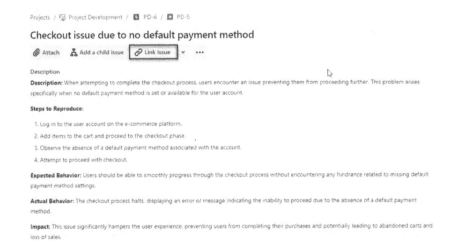

Then a section will be opened for you, select the relation of the link that you are creating

Once you have selected the relation, then select or enter the key of the issue which you want to link. The two issues in Jira will now be linked together.

In case you want to remove the linking due to any reasons, you can do it by clicking on the "x" icon on the link of this issue.

You can also create a link, while you are creating a new issue. You will see the same section of Linked Issue on the create form as well, Just select the relation and your issue. When the new issue gets created, the link will be made as well.

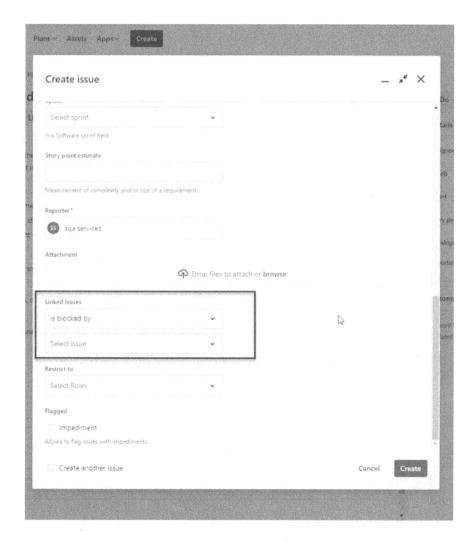

Tracking Dependencies

Dependencies, also called Issue Links in other parts of Jira, allow you to show the order in which issues need to be done. If there's a dependency between two issues, one must be finished before the next can begin.

To view the issue dependencies, go to Project timeline, from the left menu.

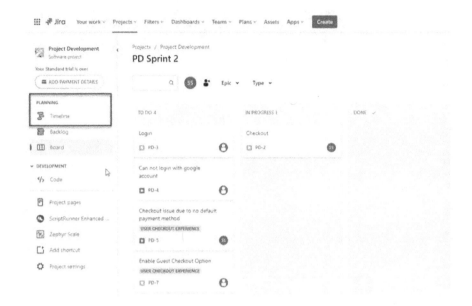

Once the project timeline is opened, expand the parent issue, and you will be able to see the dependency between the issues, based on the linking you have created.

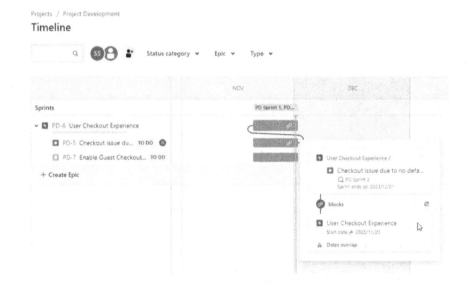

Chapter 4
Estimating in Jira

Estimation in Jira is a helpful tool for figuring out how big a to-do list is and guessing when a project/sprint might finish. Instead of guessing how long each task will take, Jira looks at the team's past work and capacity to predict when things might get done.

Once you estimate a project, you can see if your team is on track to finish by a certain date. You can also keep an eye on how the team is doing compared to what was planned.

Story Points

In Agile methodology, story points are often used for estimation. It's a unit of measure to estimate the overall effort required to implement a user story or a task. It's a relative measure of complexity, effort, and uncertainty.

By default, story points can only be assigned to story or epic-type issues, and not subtasks such as bugs. This can be changed by those with Jira administrator permissions.

Estimations Techniques

Here are some common estimation techniques used in Agile methodologies that you can implement in Jira:

Planning Poker:

Description: A collaborative technique where team members discuss and estimate the effort needed for a user story or task.

Process: Each team member independently assigns story points to the user story. Then, they reveal their estimates simultaneously. Discussion follows, especially if there's a significant difference in estimations, until a consensus is reached.

Relative Sizing:

Description: Comparing the size or effort of a user story or task relative to another known task.

Process: Team members compare the current user story to previously completed ones and assign story points based on how it relates in complexity and effort compared to those.

T-Shirt Sizing:

Description: Analogous to sizes of T-shirts (XS, S, M, L, XL), tasks or user stories are estimated based on their size relative to these sizes.

Process: Users assign story points to tasks or user stories in a way that corresponds to the size of a T-shirt. For instance, XS might represent 1-3 story points, S 3-5 points, and so on.

Fibonacci Sequence:

Description: Using the Fibonacci sequence (0, 1, 2, 3, 5, 8, 13, etc.) to assign story points.

Process: Team members assign story points from the Fibonacci sequence to tasks or user stories based on their complexity. Larger numbers indicate higher complexity or uncertainty.

How to add story points against a user story in Jira

Open the Jira and Navigate to the project. Once you are at the project, Open the issue on which you want to add story points in Jira/

On the issue screen, you would be able to see the Story point estimate field. Just click on it and enter your estimate.

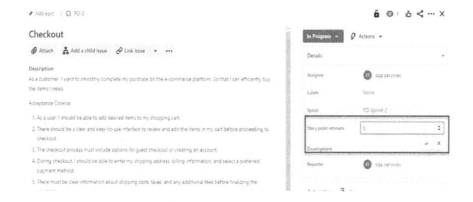

Time Tracking

Time tracking in Jira allows teams to monitor the time spent on tasks, measure progress, and compare it against the original story point estimates. Here's how you can track time and progress in Jira:

1. **Logging Work**: Jira enables users to log time spent on tasks. Team members can manually log their work hours against specific issues or user stories. They can also add comments to describe the work done.

2. **Worklogs and Comments**: When team members log work, it generates worklogs that capture details such as who worked on the task, when the work was done, and any comments or descriptions added. These logs provide a record of time spent.

3. **Time Tracking Reports**: Jira offers various reports like Burndown Charts, Sprint Reports, and Time Tracking Reports. These summarise logged work against original estimates, allowing teams to visualise progress.

How to enable time tracking on issue types in Jira

1. Go to your project and click on Project settings

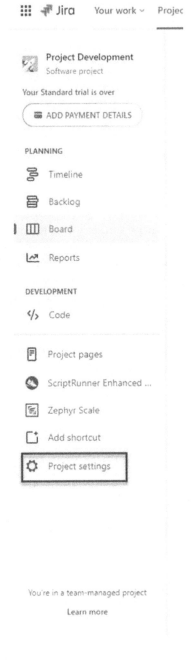

2. Click on Issue Types screen

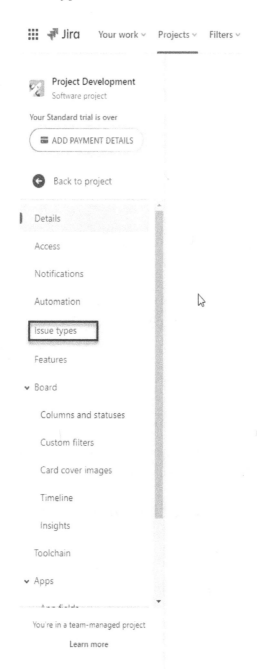

On the issue type screen, you will have a bunch of issue types that you can create in Jira, now select your issue and search for the time tracking field, if it is not already added on the screen.

Once you find the field, click on the field to add it on the issue type screen, and then click save changes.

The settings will be saved and now you will be able to see the time tracking on the issue type screen on which you have added the field.

How to add the original time spent on an issue in Jira

1. Open the issue type in Jira, on which you want to add the estimate. (Note: make sure that the time tracking field is added on the issue type screen in Jira. See the above section)

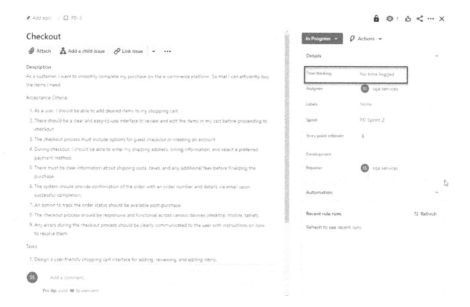

2. Click on the Time Tracking field, and the pop up will be opened to add the time that has been spent and time remaining on the issue progress.

3. Make sure to enter the date, time and work description while you are logging the time.

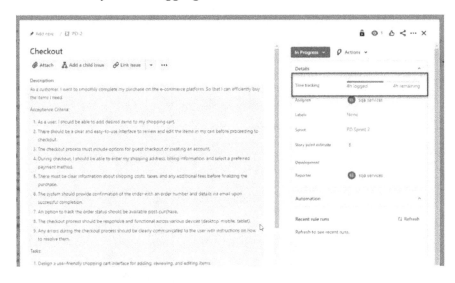

4. Once you are done, click on Save.

The time will be logged and you will be able to see the progress on the issue, in terms of the time spent vs the time remaining.

Note: It is advisable to log the time correctly and regularly on the task, so that the progress is monitored accurately and the project stakeholders are well known with the progress.

Capacity Planning

Capacity planning involves figuring out how much time a project or task will take, checking if your team has enough time to do it, and organising the work for best results.

It's divided into two steps: capacity and planning. First, you assess how much work your team can handle without overwhelming them. Then, you prioritise tasks and schedule work to meet deadlines.

Capacity planning is a process that helps to plan the resources needed to meet capacity needs. It provides an outline of the resources required (for example, people, physical assets, and budgets) to enable organisations to achieve their objectives.

Capacity Planning Tips

Learn from the past:

After project completion, conduct a postmortem to understand where capacity challenges occurred. Identify reasons for stretched capacity and develop strategies to avoid similar issues in the future.

Open team dialogues:

Regularly discuss team workloads in team meetings to stay updated on everyone's current capacities. Document these discussions using the Roles and Responsibilities template for future reference.

Gather comprehensive project details:

Before starting a project, ensure a clear understanding of its requirements to prevent scope creep. Use structured forms or briefs to collect necessary project details and anticipate potential delays.

Effective planning starts with understanding your team's capabilities. Avoid guesswork by accurately assessing your team's capacity and planning accordingly.

How to do Capacity Planning meeting in person and document it on Confluence

1. Before you conduct the meeting, request each team member to list their weekly tasks and estimated hours spent beforehand, leveraging calendars and work-related tools for accuracy.

2. Conduct a Purposeful Team Meeting and explain the reason behind assessing bandwidth in a team meeting to encourage

openness and honesty among team members about their availability.

3. Sum up individual hours spent on all activities to determine the percentage of time allocated to projects. Discuss these figures collectively to identify areas for improvement.

4. Use the Capacity Planning Template in Jira and fill it by listing the team members, their roles, percentage of time dedicated to projects, and total weekly project hours. Group similar roles to understand overall capacity per role.

Capacity planning

🛈 Full play here: https://www.atlassian.com/team-playbook/plays

Individual time allocation

Each team member adds their weekly tasks and hours needed to this table.

Name	Task	Hours needed	% of time (Hours per tasks / weekly hours)

Team capacity for project

After completing the above, add each team members percentage of time available for a specific project and record it here.

Name	Role	% of weekly time dedicated to project	Weekly hours on project	Sum by role

Now that you have a clearer picture of the team's allocation, it'll be easier to determine staffing for future projects.

5. Lastly, utilise the insights gained to assign tasks effectively, align skills with specific projects, and prevent overburdening team members, thus reducing stress and burnout.

Chapter 5
Planning in Jira

Kanban and Scrum Boards

Kanban Board

The Kanban board in JIRA is a visual project management tool that helps teams visualise and manage work using the Kanban method. A Kanban board uses cards and columns to show work. Each card represents a task or project, and columns show different stages of work, like "To Do" or "In Progress." Limits on the number of cards in a column (WIP limits) prevent too much work at once. If a column reaches its limit, the team must finish tasks before adding more. This helps find problems and keeps work flowing smoothly.

Scrum Board

A Scrum board helps teams track their work in short sprints. The aim is to move all tasks to the "Done" section by the end of the sprint. There's no fixed way to set up a Scrum board; the team decides how to show the needed information.

Usually, the board has rows or columns to track the progress of agreed-upon work for the sprint. It might include:

- To Do: Features planned for the sprint

- In Progress: Tasks started but not finished

- In Test/Review: Completed tasks being checked

- Done: Finished tasks that passed testing

You can change lanes and columns to fit your team's needs.

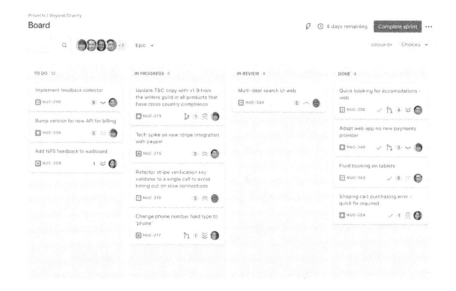

Creating and Configuring the board

Create the Board

When starting with Jira Software, follow the instructions to create your project. Usually, a board is automatically chosen for your project. So, if you follow the steps and create a Kanban/Scrum project, your board will be set up automatically.

Or if you are already using the Jira software and created a board, and want to add another board. You can go to You work > Boards > View all board from the top navigation menu

Click on Create Board

Select Kanban/Scrum board

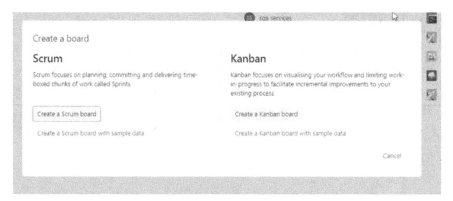

Select the most suitable option from the below and click Next

Complete the steps and in the end, your new board will be created.

Configuring the Board

When the board is created, Go to the Configure Board option from the Board screen, to manage the board as per your team needs.

Add more columns or add Work In Progress limit to columns

You can add more status columns on your board from here. Just click on "+" and add the new status column.

Also, You can edit the column name or set the maximum number of cards in any columns by clicking on the edit icon.

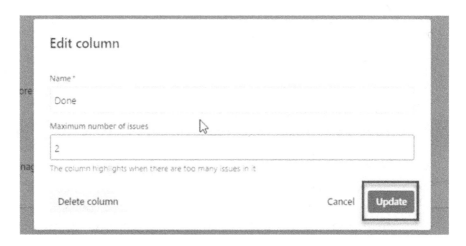

In Agile methodology, an epic in Jira is a term used to describe a large body of work that needs to be accomplished. It represents a significant and sizable piece of a project or a product, which can be broken down into smaller, manageable tasks or user stories.

Custom Filters on the Board

You can then go to the board, and select the filter to view the filtered tickets on the board.

Understanding Epics

Here are some key points about Agile Jira epics:

- **Size and Scope**: Epics are substantial in size and scope, often too big to be completed in a single iteration or sprint. They cover a broad area of functionality or a large user need within a project.

- **Dividing into User Stories**: Epics are further broken down into smaller, more manageable user stories or tasks. These stories are the actionable items that teams work on within the sprint.

- **Cross-Team or Cross-Project**: Epics can span multiple teams, projects, or even departments. They serve as a unifying element, aligning the efforts of various teams towards a common goal.

- **Tracking and Management**: Jira, a popular project management tool, allows teams to create, track, and manage epics. They can be visualised on boards, providing a clear overview of the progress and status of the work related to the epic.

- **Adaptability**: Epics are dynamic and adaptable. As teams progress through the development process and gather feedback, they can add, remove, or reprioritize user stories within the epic based on changing requirements or customer needs.

- **Sprint Planning**: Epics are usually too large to fit into a single sprint. Teams break them down into smaller tasks or stories that can be completed within individual sprints while continuously working towards the larger epic's completion.

- **Visibility and Communication**: Epics offer visibility to stakeholders and team members about the overall progress and direction of a project. They facilitate communication and collaboration among different teams working on interconnected tasks.

How to create Epics in Jira

There are three ways to create epics in Jira Software, from the Timeline, Backlog, and using the Global Create issue button. When you create an epic, you'll need to enter the following details:

- **Epic name** - A short identifier for your epic. This will be used as a label on issues that belong to this epic.

- **Epic summary** - You'll see this whenever Jira displays the epic.

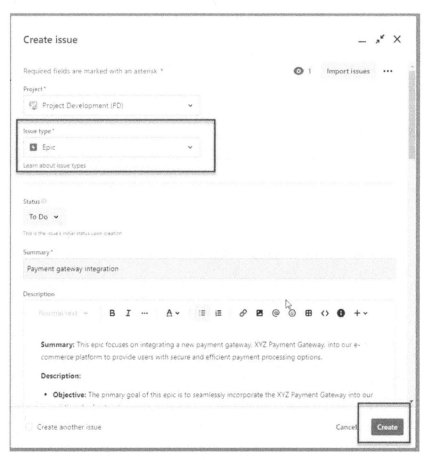

Create user stories against the epic

After you have created the epic, You can then break the epic into multiple user stories in Jira to break down the big tasks into smaller ones.

In order to do this, go to the epic issue type, click on the Add Child Issue button, Select the type as User Story and give it a title.

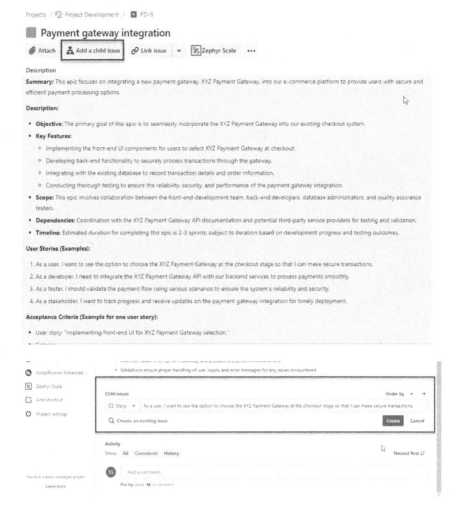

The epic can be then broken down into smaller tasks that can be achieved in the sprints.

Track the epic details

You can view an epic's details, like start date, due date, and child issues by selecting the epic in the timeline or backlog.

Closing the Epic

Once all the work for an epic is completed, you should mark it as complete on the timeline.

To complete an epic:

1. Navigate to the Timeline.

2. Select the epic you'd like to mark as complete.

3. Under Status, select Done.

Mark your epic as Done whenever all work for the epic is complete. To make this easier, we recommend coming up with a clear definition of done for your epic when you create it. Child-issues don't have to be complete to mark an epic as done.

Organising Work on Backlogs

The backlog is like a to-do list for your team's tasks. It shows the work your team will do soon and later.

In the backlog, you see a list of tasks planned for the future (in the Backlog or Sprint lists) and those currently on your team's board (in the Board list). It helps plan work ahead so your team can tackle important tasks promptly when they're prepared.

Usually, teams using Kanban style don't use a backlog; they manage tasks more directly without planning them in advance.

View Backlog and Add tasks in it

To create issues for your team to work on in your backlog:

1. Navigate to your team-managed Jira Software project.

2. In your project's sidebar, select Backlog.

3. Scroll to the bottom of your Backlog list and select + Create issue.

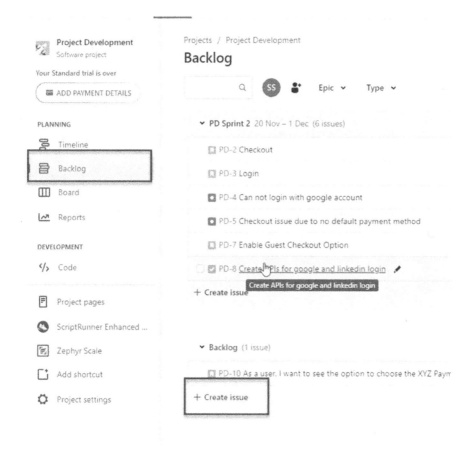

When you add a new task, It is added to the backlog, if you do not assign a sprint to it. You can then move the tasks from the backlog to the Sprint section, as seen in the above screenshot.

Prioritising the work in the backlog

Prioritising your backlog is an important step in backlog management. This ensures that the most important items are tackled first, and the team is working on the items that will have the biggest impact on the project. Jira Software provides several ways to prioritise your backlog:

- **Drag and Drop**: You can drag and drop items in the backlog to reorder them based on priority. Simply click and hold the item, and drag it to the desired position in the list.

- **Priority Field (recommended)**: Jira Software allows you to set a priority field for each item in the backlog. This field can be used to rank items based on their importance.

- **Ranking Field**: Jira Software also provides a ranking field that allows you to rank items based on their importance. This field can be used to override the priority field if necessary.

Labelling the Backlog items

There are several ways to define the requests to be processed in your backlog. Some of them are;

- Create a specific label to manage your backlog. Some examples: "for backlog", "validated", or conversely, "frozen", "not taken into account", etc.

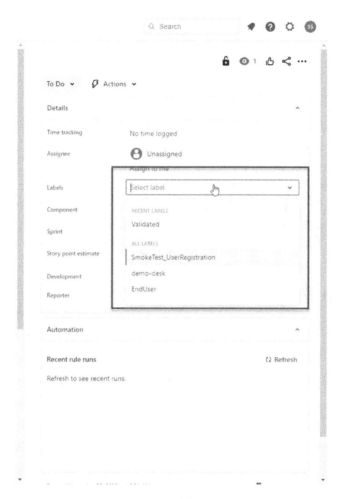

- Create a component or a custom field and use the logic that suits you the best. Component examples: "Out of scope", "Validated", "For development".

NOTE: We have added this custom field of component, which we will cover later.

Whichever option you choose, keep in mind that you are creating a filter to see requests, which must be present in the backlog.

In summary, handling a backlog might seem tricky, but with the proper tools and methods, it gets simpler. Jira Software is great for managing backlogs. By using the steps in this guide, you can make your backlog fit your team's needs. When you put the most important tasks first, keep an eye on how things are going, and adjust your backlog view, your team can focus on what matters most and move towards reaching your project goals

Planning Work in Sprints

Before starting a sprint, your Scrum team usually has a meeting to plan. In this meeting, the team:

- Check how much time tasks might take.

- Splits tasks into smaller parts for the sprint.

- Think about days off and other things that might affect finishing tasks.

- Figures out if the team has enough time to finish all the tasks.

By the end of the meeting, the team feels sure they can finish the work they've planned for the sprint.

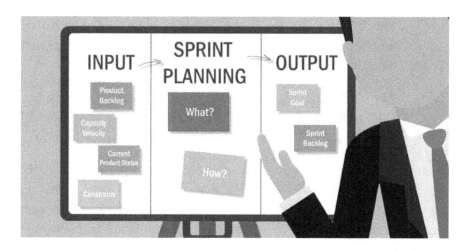

The sprint planning session is crucial for starting the sprint on the right track. It sets the goals and direction for the team. When done well, it motivates and challenges the team to succeed. However, a poorly planned sprint can cause problems by creating unrealistic expectations.

Here's a breakdown of what happens during sprint planning:

- **The What**: The product owner outlines the sprint's objective and which tasks from the backlog contribute to it. The team then decides what they can accomplish during the sprint to reach that goal.

- **The How**: The development team plans the work needed to achieve the sprint goal. The final plan is a negotiation between the development team and the product owner, considering value and effort.

- **The Who**: Both the product owner and the development team are essential for sprint planning. The product owner defines the goal based on value, while the development team figures out how they can achieve it. Missing either of them makes planning nearly impossible.

- **The Inputs**: The product backlog provides a starting point for the sprint plan. It's also essential to consider the existing work and the team's capacity.

- **The Outputs**: The main outcome of sprint planning is a clear understanding of the sprint goal and how the team will work towards it. This is documented in the sprint backlog.

For a successful sprint planning meeting, preparation is key. The product owner needs to be ready with insights from previous reviews, stakeholder feedback, and a clear product vision. Keeping an updated and refined product backlog enhances transparency and clarity.

A helpful tip is to consider a backlog refinement meeting midway through a two-week sprint. This helps the team step back, review what's next, and gain fresh perspectives, aiding both sprint planning preparation and the ongoing work.

Creating and managing the Sprints

In Jira, a sprint is like a short, focused burst of activity where your team tackles a set of prioritised tasks from the product backlog. Think of it as a mini-project within a larger project, with a clear beginning and end.

Imagine a race with short laps, not one long run. Each lap is a "sprint" where teams build a small part of the final product.

- Before the sprint: They plan what to build (from a list called the "backlog").

- During the sprint: They work hard to finish that part.

- After the sprint: They show what they built and adjust their plans for the next lap.

Jira Software helps them plan each lap, making it easier and faster.

Create a sprint in Jira

Open and access your project in Jira, and navigate to the Backlog screen.

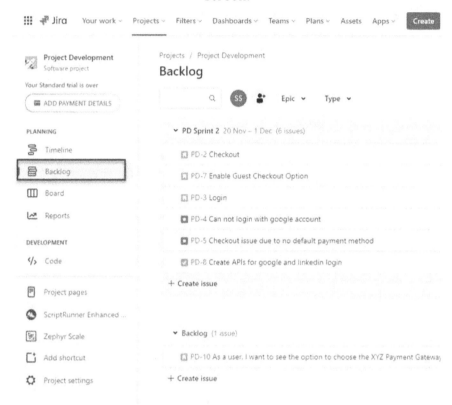

On the backlog screen, You will see the Create Sprint button, which allows you to create a new sprint.

When you click on it, a new sprint will be created. After that click on Add dates.

On the dialog box, you can name the sprint, add the dates of the sprint and save the details.

Your sprint is now ready in Jira, The next step is to add the issues from Backlog in the Sprint.

Adding issues to the sprint backlog

There are two ways through which you can add the issues in the sprint.

One is, from the backlog screen, you can drag and move the issues from the Backlog section to the Sprint section and the issues will be added in the Sprint.

Second method allows you to assign the sprint to the issue from the Issue screen. For that, Open the issue in detail view which you want to add to the sprint.

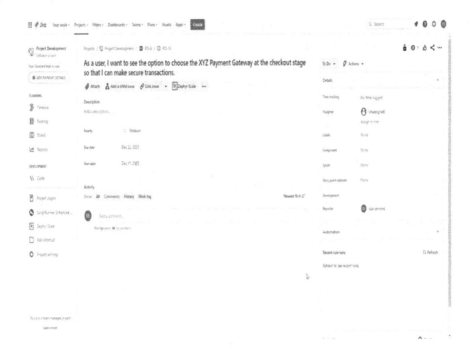

On the right side, you can see the Sprint column, click on it and you will be able to see all the sprints added in the project. Select the sprint and the issues will be added in the selected sprint.

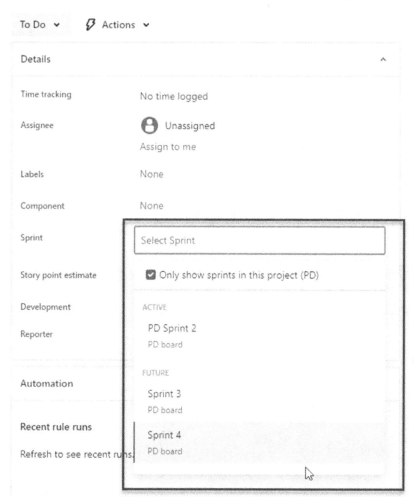

Starting the sprint

On the board, locate and click on the "+ Create sprint" button. This action will prompt a window where you can define the details of the sprint.

Once you have added the details, click on the Start button to start the sprint.

Monitor Sprint Progress

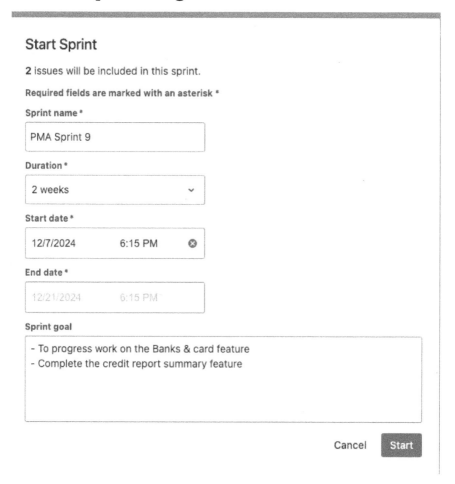

Start Sprint

2 issues will be included in this sprint.

Required fields are marked with an asterisk *

Sprint name *

PMA Sprint 9

Duration *

2 weeks

Start date *

12/7/2024   6:15 PM

End date *

12/21/2024   6:15 PM

Sprint goal

- To progress work on the Banks & card feature
- Complete the credit report summary feature

Cancel   Start

- **Monitor Board:** Once the sprint starts, the team can visualise the sprint's progress on the board. Tasks will move across columns (e.g., To Do, In Progress, Done) as they're worked on and completed.

- **Daily Stand-ups:** Conduct regular stand-up meetings where the team discusses progress, blockers, and plans for the day to ensure alignment and address any impediments.

- **Sprint Report:** Throughout the sprint, keeping tabs on the team's progress is essential. One effective method is to track it through the Sprint Report.

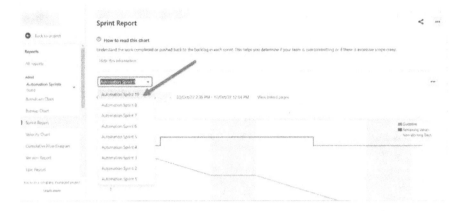

The Sprint Report maintains records of all sprints. The team can easily navigate to the drop-down menu where the list of issues and their progress (To-Do, In-Progress, or Done) will be displayed accordingly. This helps the team see the previous and current sprint status and track the progress accordingly.

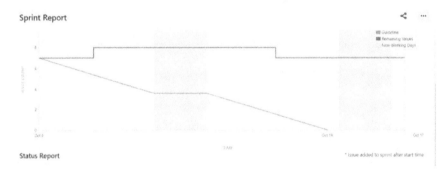

The Sprint Report chart utilises a colour-coded system to convey various statuses:

1. **White**: Denotes tasks or items that have not yet commenced or are in the "To-Do" phase.

2. **Gray**: Represents items that are presently in progress or within the "In-Progress" phase.

3. **Red**: Indicates tasks or items that have been successfully completed and reside in the "Done" phase.

This colour scheme offers a visual representation of task statuses within the sprint, facilitating a quick and intuitive assessment of progress for the team.

In a Sprint Report, "**issues not completed**" refer to tasks or items that were planned for the sprint but were not finished by the end of the sprint duration. These are typically items that remain in the **"To-Do"** or **"In-Progress"** phases.

On the other hand **"Completed issues"** are tasks or items that were successfully finished and moved to the **"Done"** phase within the specified sprint period. These are the deliverables that were achieved and met the criteria for completion as outlined during sprint planning. The Sprint Report provides a summary of both completed and outstanding issues, offering insights into the team's progress and the status of planned work items.

Completing the Sprint

To conclude a sprint:

Access the Active sprints on your Scrum board.

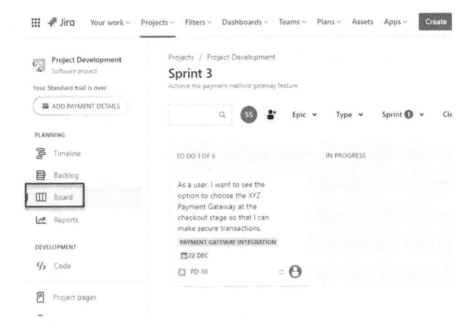

If there are multiple active sprints, choose the specific sprint from the sprint drop-down menu. The 'Complete Sprint' button will only appear after selecting a sprint.

Click on 'Complete Sprint'. This action will move all completed issues out of Active sprints.

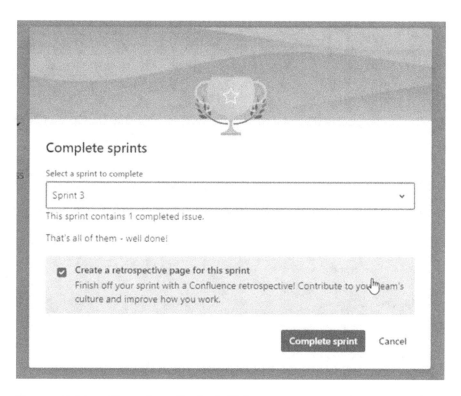

Upon clicking 'Complete Sprint', if there are remaining incomplete issues, you'll be prompted to move them to one of the following options:

- The backlog

- Any upcoming future sprint

- Create a new sprint

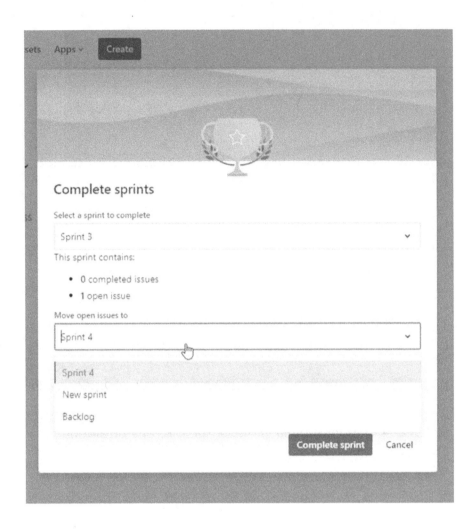

Refining Sprints and Backlog

Backlog refinement means going through, organising, and improving your list of tasks and goals for a product. It's really important because it helps the team focus on creating only what the customers want and what the business actually needs.

Who does the backlog refinement?

This refining of the backlog is continuous and involves the product owner, product managers, scrum master, business analysts, and some team members who work on development.

Sprint planning vs Backlog refinement

Sprint planning and backlog refinement go hand in hand. Backlog refinement makes sure the list of tasks reflects what we've learned from customers and what's important for the business. During sprint planning, the development team chooses tasks from the backlog to work on in the next sprint and commits to finishing them.

How to do Backlog refinement?

Teams work best when they work together on the backlog regularly. It's important to refine the backlog before each planning meeting, which usually happens every two weeks. This process takes around 30 minutes for most teams. The product owner manages the backlog, and they also update it as they learn more and get feedback from customers and the business.

1. Navigate to the backlog. In the backlog view, you can drag and drop the issues into a rough priority order.

2. Issues at the top of the backlog list should include relevant details, like time estimates and assignee, so they're ready for action in the next sprint.

3. Delete duplicate issues and break work into subtasks as needed.

4. Before closing out, confirm your priority ranking. The prioritised backlog guides the focus of your next sprint planning meeting.

Managing Release Backlogs and Sprint Backlogs

- **Release backlog**: Features that need to be implemented for a particular release

- **Sprint backlog**: User stories that need to be completed during a specific period of time

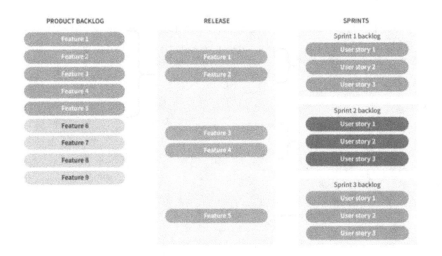

How to create and manage sprint backlog

We have already seen that in the above section, In case you want to go through it again, click here.

How to create and manage release backlog.

Enable the releases feature in project

Before creating the release, ensure that the "Releases" feature is enabled in your jira project. For that, navigate to the project settings.

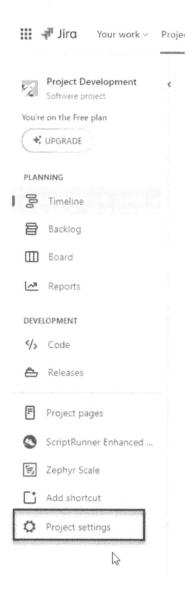

Under the features section, enable the Releases feature.

Now you will be able to see the Releases menu item in the left menu.

Create the release version

Go to releases from the left menu bar, and click to create a new release version.

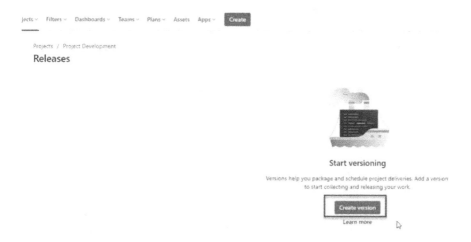

Add the release details and click on the save button to create the release.

Your release will now be created.

Adding the features into the release

Go to the release details. And click on the "+" icon to add the releases.

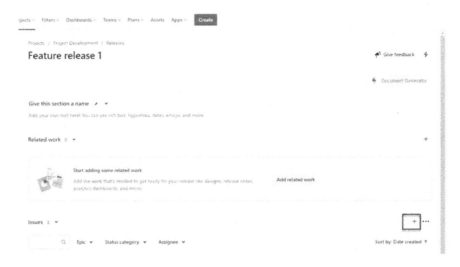

Now add all the tasks, user stories and features that are going to be shipped in this release.

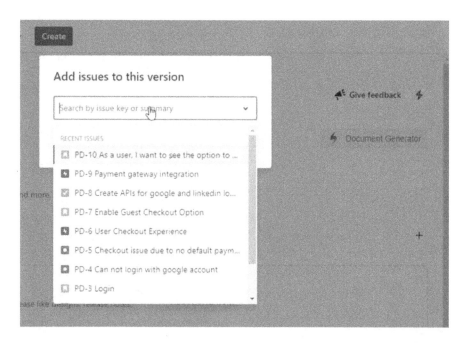

Once you have added all the tasks in the release, click on Add to add the items in the release.

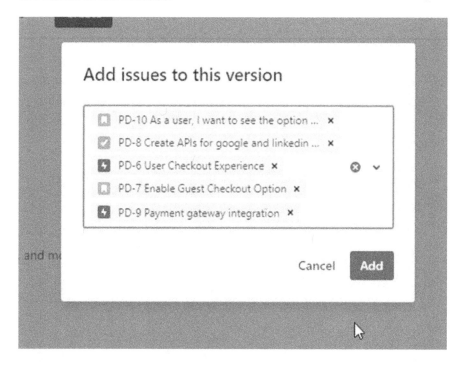

Managing the release:

You can track the progress of the release items from the section, highlighted below.

And once your release is ready to be shipped, you can change the status of the release to "Released".

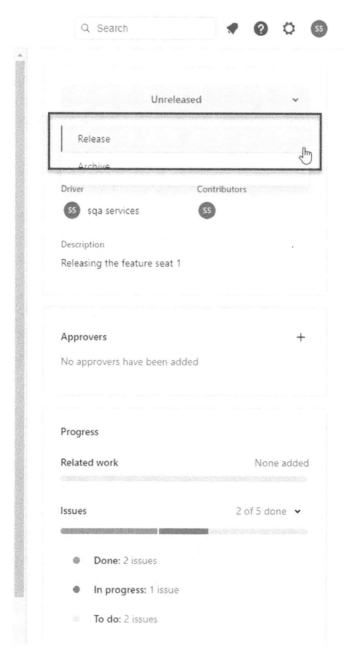

Before you change the status to Release, you will be asked to create the release notes for the release. Either you can create it in Confluence or in Jira itself.

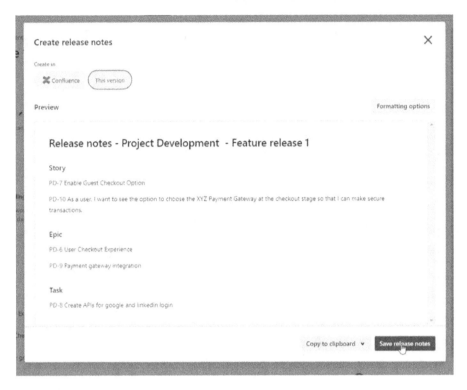

Click on Save release notes to save it and proceed.

Now the release you created, has been released in Jira and to the client.

Released ✓

Start date
December 11. 2023

Release date
December 29. 2023

Driver
sqa services

Contributors

Description
Releasing the feature seat 1

Approvers +

No approvers have been added

Progress

Related work 1 of 1 added

Issues 2 of 5 done ✓

• **Done:** 2 issues

• **In progress:** 1 issue

○ **To do:** 2 issues

Chapter 6
Issue Tracking and Management

Searching and Filtering Issues

Creating issues is important, and it's equally as important to be able to search and manage multiple issues to ensure you and your team work together well. You can search for the issues in JIRA with different ways, which are mentioned below;

Quick Search

The quick search is the fastest way to define search criteria. It is most useful when your search criteria is not complex, for example, you know the project key and some keywords for an issue.

To perform a quick search, open your project in JIRA and type in your search keywords at the search bar on the top and you will get the results with the matching keywords.

Basic Search

The basic search is more precise than the quick search, but easier to use than the advanced search. It provides a user-friendly interface that lets you define complex queries, without needing to know how to use JQL (advanced searching).

To perform a basic search, open your project in JIRA and click on the search bar at the top, It will open a pop up, from there click on the View All Issue button.

It will open the screen for advanced search like this.

From here, you can select and add the filter in your search, and search through their values. For example, if I want to search all the user stories from a specific project, I will select my project value from the project drop down.

After that, I will apply the filter on Issue type and select the value as User Story.

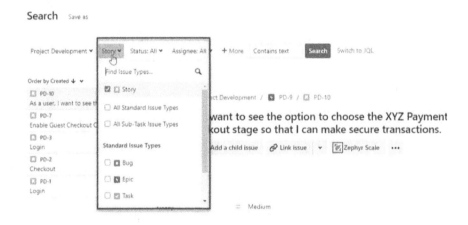

Note: I can select more than 1 value here, But for my example scenario, I am using one search filter and value.

In return, This search will get me all the user stories from the selected project.

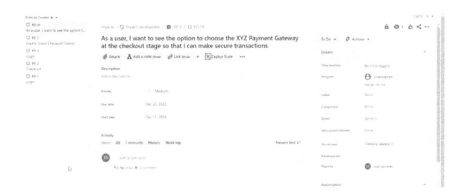

I can add more filters by clicking on More and selecting the fields I want to apply filters on.

Advanced Search

The advanced search is the most powerful of the three search methods. You can specify criteria that cannot be defined in the other searches (e.g. ORDER BY clause). However, you need to know how to construct structured queries using the Jira Query Language (JQL) to use this feature.

We will see more of it in the later section, in this chapter.

Creating and Saving Filters

If you frequently run the same search, you can save the search criteria as a filter. This saves you from having to manually redefine the search criteria every time.

Jira applications also include a number of predefined system filters for common queries, such as 'My Open Issues', 'Reported by Me', 'Recently Viewed', and 'All Issues'.

Save your search as a filter:

On the search results page, click Save as and enter a name for the filter.

Your new filter will be shown in the left panel with your other favourite filters, filters shared with you, and the system filters. To run a filter, just click it.

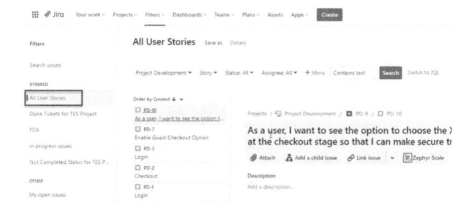

Bulk Issue Changes

At some point, you may need to change multiple issues at the same time. You can do this by performing a Bulk Change operation.

For example: You may want to assign Release Version to all the tickets in the sprint. Rather than you do it manually on all tickets, one by one, you can use Bulk Operation to update all tickets at once.

In order to do the Bulk changes, Go to Advanced search issue by clicking on View All Issue after you click on the search issue bar at the top header.

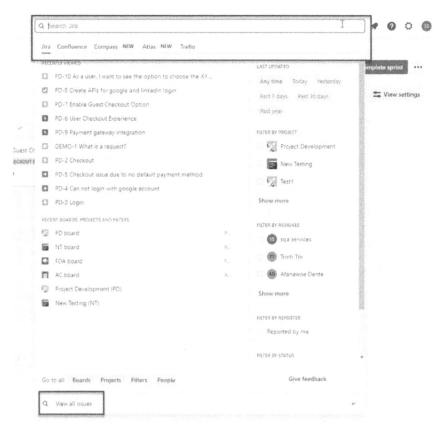

Once you are on the advanced search screen, you can see the three dots highlighted in the screenshot below, Click on it and select the Bulk change all issue option.

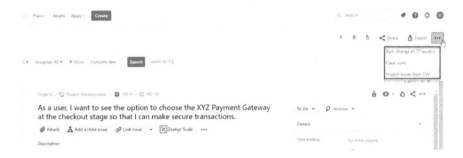

When you click on it, It will redirect you to the screen, where all the issues (as per the filter you have selected on the Advanced search screen issues) will be displayed, and from there you can select all or select some specific issues which you want to update.

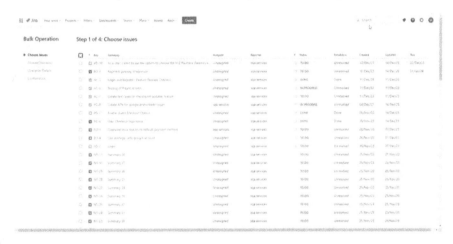

After you select the issue, on which you want to perform the update, Click Next.

Now select the bulk operation which you want to perform, you can select any option from the following, which are listed on the screen.

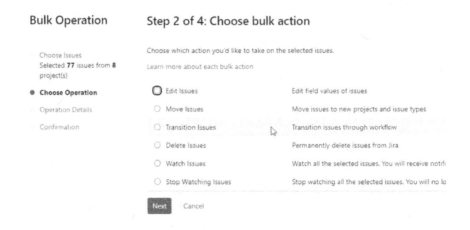

For now, I will select the edit issue option, and click next.

Now you will get a list of all fields that you can change/update on all issues. You can select that, make changes and click save.

For this, I am changing the assignee to all tickets and initiating the bulk change.

Step 3 of 4: Operation Details

Note: You can choose to deselect Send mail for this update option when you choose what to update for the issues. This avoids notification overload for everyone working on the issues being edited. Notifications, if sent, will likely go to anyone watching an affected issue.

On the next step, Before the bulk change is initiated, review the changes. If all is good, Click on confirm button and all the changes will be done. *NOTE: To perform a bulk operation, you'll need the global Make bulk changes permission and the relevant permission for each project. For example, you would need to have the Move Issue project permission and Make bulk changes global permissions to move a group of issues at the same time.*

Click on the Acknowledge button and then you will be redirected to the issue search screen where you can review the changes that were done.

Jira Query Language (JQL)

JQL stands for Jira Query Language and is the most powerful and flexible way to search for your issues in Jira. JQL is for everyone: developers, testers, agile project managers, and business users.

JQL Format

JQL Queries are like puzzles made of simple pieces. Each query has three main parts: fields (like types of information), operators (which connect the pieces), and values (the actual things you're searching for).

- **Fields**: These are different kinds of information in Jira, such as priority or issue type.

- **Operators**: These are like the glue that connects the fields to what you're looking for. For example, equals (=), not equals (!=), or less than (<).

- **Values**: These are the actual things you're searching for, like a specific priority level or an issue type.

- **Keywords**: These are special words like AND and OR that help combine different parts of the query.

Basic JQL queries

To run the JQL Queries, go to advanced search issue and click on Switch to JQL.

Now write any of the below queries to run some basic and sample queries.

- 'project = "My Project"': This will return all issues in the "My Project" project.

- 'assignee = currentUser()': This will return all issues assigned to the currently logged-in user.

- 'status = "In Progress":' This will return all issues with the status "In Progress".

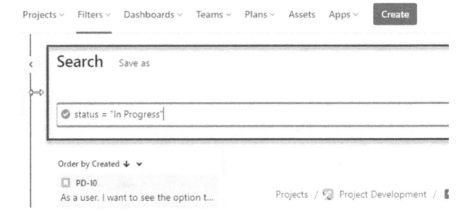

Advanced JQL Queries

Advanced JQL usage often involves combining multiple conditions within a single query. You can do this using logical operators such as 'AND', 'OR', and 'NOT'.

For instance, suppose you want to find all open or in-progress issues assigned to you. Your JQL query might look like this: 'status = "In Progress" AND assignee = currentUser()'. This query uses the AND operator to combine two conditions: the issue's status and its assignee status = "In Progress" AND assignee = currentUser()

Bonus: You can download the official JQL Cheat sheet from here. https://atlassianblog.wpengine.com/wp-content/uploads/2022/03/atlassian-jql-cheat-sheet-2.pdf

Dashboards and Gadgets

Jira Dashboards

Jira dashboard is like a customizable workspace where teams can check their project progress and status easily. It shows important project information in one place using different tools like charts and lists. Teams can change or add these tools to fit their needs.

A big advantage of the Jira dashboard is that it gives real-time updates about project progress.

How to navigate to Jira Dashboards?

To view all of your dashboards, choose Dashboards > View all dashboards.

How to create your first Dashboard in Jira?

In order to create your first dashboard, Go to your project and;

1. Choose Dashboards > Create Dashboards.

2. Name your dashboard and add a description so your team knows when to use it.

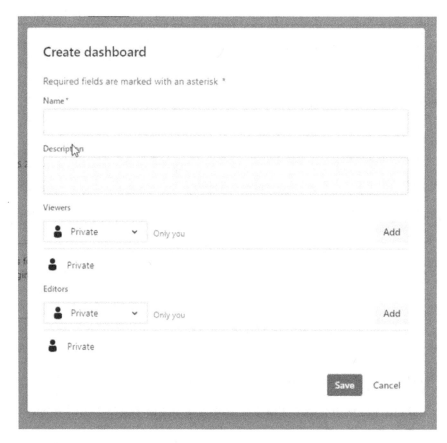

3. Fill out the remaining fields and click Save.

Congrats! You have created your first Jira dashboard.

Adding gadgets to your Jira Dashboard

Next, you'll see the dashboard settings. Here, you can put useful tools on your empty dashboard by clicking "Add gadget." Jira offers many tools like charts and visual aids to help with your dashboard.

For example, if It want to add a dashboard that can show me the tickets that are assigned to me and update it after 15 minutes, I will use "Assigned to Me" gadget, that is by default provided by Jira.

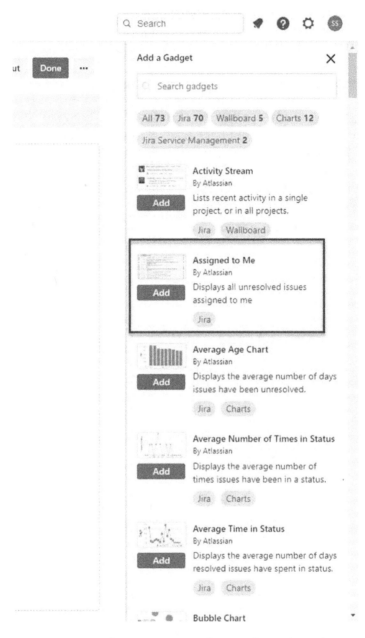

Now configure the gadget by setting the number of results you want to display, which columns you want to see (like Issue name, type, summary, status), select or deselect auto refresh and click Save.

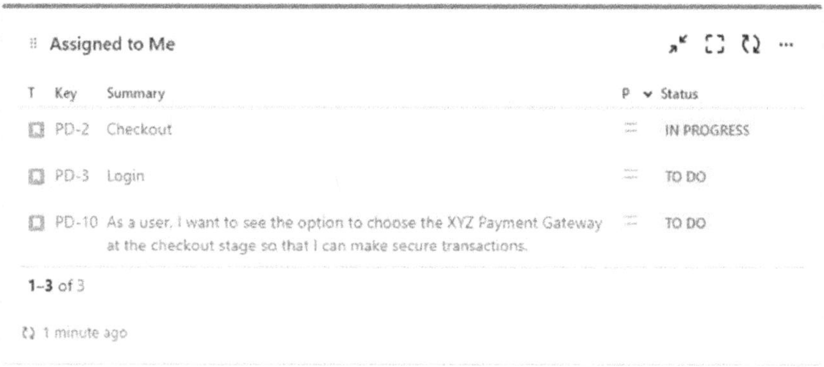

⁑ Assigned to Me

T	Key	Summary	P	⌄	Status
▣	PD-2	Checkout	≕		IN PROGRESS
▣	PD-3	Login	≕		TO DO
▣	PD-10	As a user, I want to see the option to choose the XYZ Payment Gateway at the checkout stage so that I can make secure transactions.	≕		TO DO

1–3 of 3

↻ 1 minute ago

Your gadget will be created successfully and it will start showing some data.

You can also create the dashboard for the customised requirements. For that, You will have to create a filter, which we have seen here.

To create a dashboard for a filter, add a gadget like "Filter results"

After that, you will be asked to select the Saved filter from which the gadget will read the data. Along with that, set the configurations and click Save.

Now you will be displayed all the issue types as per the filter criteria that you have created.

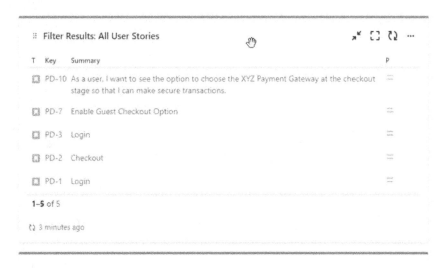

Changing the layout for your dashboard

You will be prompted to choose a layout for your dashboard. Jira provides several layout options to choose from, including two, three, and four-column layouts. Choose the layout that best suits your needs.

Sharing the dashboard with Team

Users in Jira can easily share their personal dashboards with team members, stakeholders, or external partners. This sharing feature makes it simple for everyone involved to access and stay updated on important project details, promoting effective collaboration.

Navigate to the Dashboard page.

Click on the three dots button at the top right corner

You will see a dialog box, from where you can rename the dashboard or set the sharing settings.

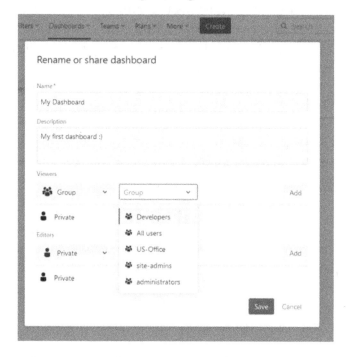

Users can choose several permission levels from the menu. You can share it with:

- Users who are working on the same Project

- Share the dashboard with a specific Group (team)

- Share on the level of the whole Organisation

- Share it with a certain User

- or make it Private.

Similarly, you can set the same settings for the editors of the project.

Creating Labels in Jira

One of its most handy features is the ability to add labels to issues. Labels are keywords or phrases that you can add to issues to categorise and track them. This makes it easy to find all the issues that are related to a certain topic.

For example, you could add the label "login" to all of the issues that are login-related, or you could add the label "frontend" to all of the issues that affect the frontend. You can also add multiple labels to an issue, which can be helpful if you need to track multiple things, say login problems that become apparent in the frontend.

How to add/create label on an issue

1. Open an issue that you want to add a label to.

2. Click on the label field.

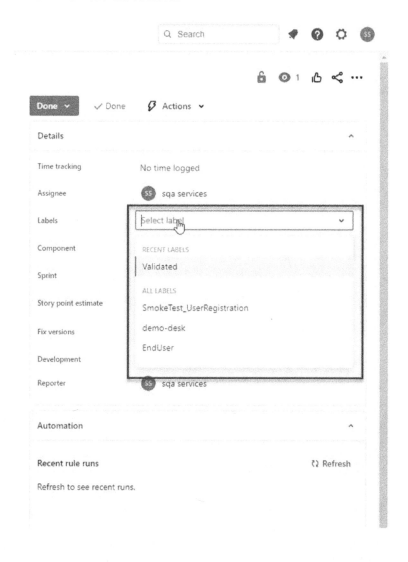

3. Start typing! Jira will suggest labels that are already in use in your instance, making it easy to stay consistent.

4. Hit enter when you are done, or pick an existing from the list.

You can assign more than one label to any one issue.

How to remove a label from an issue

Deleting a label is just as simple. Again, open the issue in question, click into the label field and then click the X next to the label you want to delete:

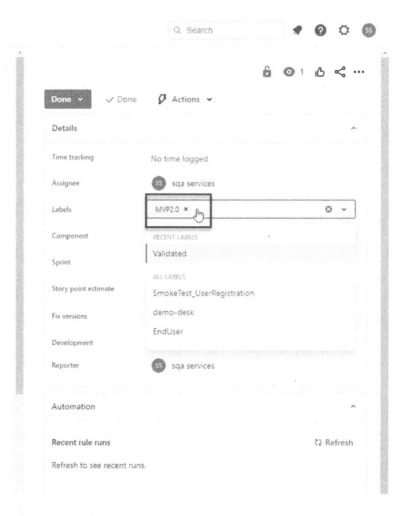

Issues to avoid while creating labels in Jira

Here are some common issues to watch out for when using labels in Jira:

- **Misspelt Labels**: Jira suggests labels as you type, but if a misspelt label is used once, it sticks around in suggestions until it's removed from all issues. This could Spread the misspelling. So, it's smart to keep an eye on your team's label use and correct any mistakes.

- **Unclear Labels**: Labels are quick to add, but they don't give a lot of detail. Make sure labels are easy to understand on their own. For instance, "frontend" is clear, but "fe" isn't. Avoid using project keys in labels too.

- **Too Many Labels**: Having lots of labels isn't always good. As the number grows, it's easier to introduce mistakes or confusing labels. This might mean needing more label management.

Building and Customising Workflows

All Jira projects contain issues that your team can view, work on, and transition through stages of work — from creation to completion. The path that your issues take is called a workflow. Each Jira workflow is composed of a set of:

- statuses (the state your work can be in)

- and transitions (how your work moves between statuses)

that your issue moves through during its lifecycle, and typically represents work processes within your organisation.

Here is an example of default workflow in Jira:

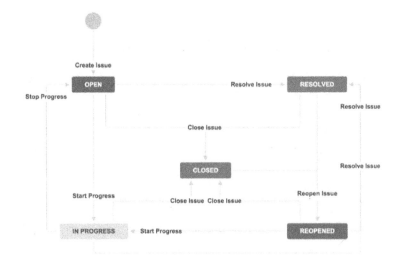

Workflow status and transitions

A status represents the state of an issue at a specific point in your workflow (e.g. "In progress"). An issue can be in only one status at a given point in time. When defining a status, you can specify properties if needed.

A transition is a link between two statuses that enables an issue to move from one status to another. To move an issue between two statuses, a transition must exist.

How to Create or Manage workflow?

By default there will be a simple workflow created and configured for your project in Jira, which will allow you to change the status of a ticket from any status to Done or moving back from Done status to In progress or To Do status.

To open and review the workflow, we need to open the workflow editor. In order to do that, Go to the project screen, click on the three dots at the right corner and click on Manage Workflow.

This will redirect you to the workflow editor screen, where you can see the default workflow.

145

You can make changes to the workflow or you can create your own workflow. For example, if we want to implement a business rule like for every issue in To Do, it must go to In Progress first and then go to Done from In Progress.

In order to achieve that, first we will remove existing transitions. Click on the arrow going towards the status box, and press the Delete key from the keyboard and the transition will be removed. Similarly, we will do this for all.

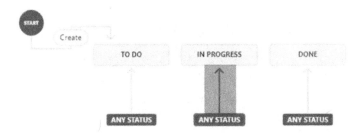

Once all the transitions are removed, We will create a new transition, By clicking on the Transition button.

On the create transition dialog box, select the From Status and To status and give this transition a name then click create.

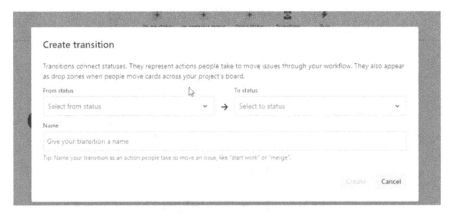

Your transition will be created. Similarly, we will do this for the complete workflow, and in the end you will have workflow created as per the business processes.

Click on the Update workflow button to save and activate the workflow.

You will be then asked to activate the workflow on the given issue types. You can select all or some.

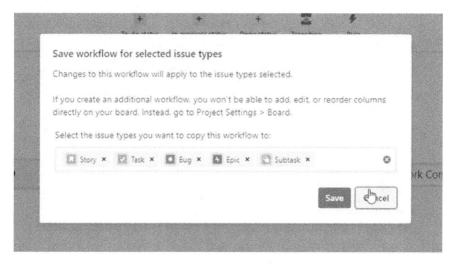

Now after saving the workflow, If I am making a transition of an issue from To Do status to any other status, It is only showing me the possible transition to In Progress only, because we created a workflow that an issue can not be moved from To do to Done.

Best Practices to create workflows

Teams using Jira can use workflows to organise complex tasks. Here are tips for effective workflow use:

- **Keep It Simple**: Don't make workflows overly complicated. Focus on the essentials needed for your project.

- **Match Workflows to Real Processes**: Design workflows based on actual business operations, not just theoretical ideas. Ensure your team can execute each step as defined.

- **Involve Everyone**: Get input from all involved parties before creating a workflow. Consider the needs of everyone affected by the workflow's outcomes.

- **Use Clear Diagrams**: Make workflow diagrams easy to understand with clear visuals and colour coding.

- **Test Workflows**: Before rolling out a workflow, test it. Keep testing intermittently even after implementation to spot issues and improve the process.

Chapter 7
Tracking Progress in Jira

Understanding Issue and Task Statuses

The status of an issue shows where it stands in the project's workflow. When you create a new project from our templates, default statuses are generated. These statuses serve as initial recommendations for each template, yet they're customizable — you can modify or delete them according to your team's requirements. Additionally, you have the option to create new statuses.

Here's a list of the statuses that come with JIRA products, depending on what projects you've created on your site.

- **Open**: The issue is open and ready for the assignee to start work on it.

- **In Progress**: This issue is being actively worked on at the moment by the assignee.

- **Done**: Work has finished on the issue.

- **To Do**: The issue has been reported and is waiting for the team to action it.

How to Create a new issue status in Jira Software

Go to your Jira project and navigate to the Board screen. Click on the "+" icon to add a new status for your issues

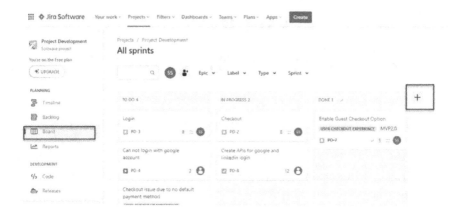

Name the new status that you want to add press enter key or click on the ✅ icon.

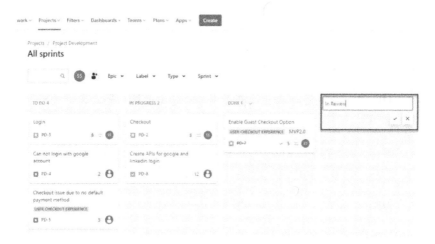

The new status will be added.

How to configure the new issue status in Workflow

To incorporate the new issue status in the workflow of statuses in your project, click on the three dots at the top right corner on the board screen, and click on manage workflow button.

You will be able to see the new status on the workflow editor screen, Now you can set up the workflow as per your business needs and save it.

How to delete an issue status

Go to the project board, and hover the mouse over the status that you want to delete. Click on the three dots on that specific issue status, to open the menu. From the menu options, click on the Delete button.

Now you will be shown a pop up that will ask for confirmation and about moving the work from the status that you are about to delete. Select the relevant configuration and click on the Delete button.

The issue will be now deleted.

Workflow and Resolution Statuses

As we have learned about the workflows in the earlier chapter and sections, let's figure out about Resolution statuses here.

The "Resolution" field is an important feature in Jira. It specifies the reason an issue is closed and removes the need of having multiple statuses with the purpose of stating why the issue is closed, thus capturing important data for your team while reducing the time you have to manage your workflow.

Here's the issues resolutions that come with your Jira products by default:

- **Done**: Work has been completed on this issue.

- **Won't do**: This issue won't be actioned.

- **Duplicate**: The problem is a duplicate of an existing issue.

An issue with a resolution will look like the following picture, where you can see its resolution next to the status name:

Resolutions configuration for team-managed projects

In Team Managed Projects like Service or Software Projects, manually setting or viewing the Resolution field isn't possible. This field isn't supported for such projects. However, a workaround involves creating an Automation Rule—either globally for all Team-Managed projects or at the team level. This rule would automatically set the Resolution field when an issue transitions to a 'Done' status in Jira. The rule's purpose is to ensure that once an issue reaches completion, the Resolution field is automatically set, maintaining a consistent resolution for all completed issues.

We will look into the details of Jira automation more in the next chapter.

Burndowns and Burnups

Burn up chart

The Burnup Chart provides a visual representation of a sprint's completed work compared with its total scope. It offers insights on your project's progress, as well as offers warnings to help you maintain your project's health; you can instantly identify problems such as scope creep or a deviation from the planned project path.

1. To view the burn up chart, Click Projects then select the relevant project.

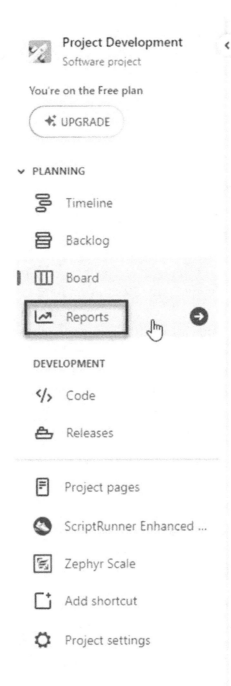

2. Click Reports, then select Burnup Chart.

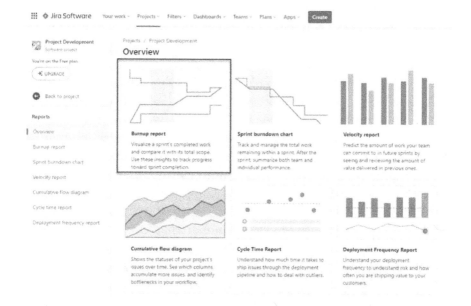

   a. To choose a different sprint, or a different measurement for the vertical axis, simply click the drop-down menus.

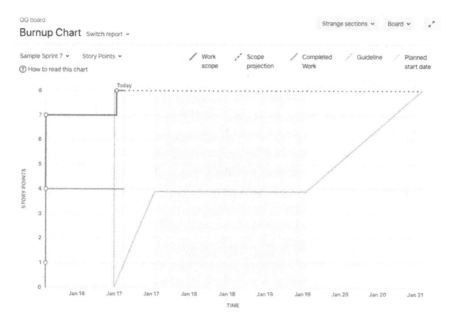

- The vertical axis represents the amount of work, and can be measured in different ways such as story points, issue count, or estimates. The horizontal axis represents time in days.

- The chart shows the red work scope line and the green completed work line (completed stories, tasks, fixed incidents for example) in relation to the grey Guideline, which is a theoretical line showing the daily completion necessary to meet the deadline.The distance between the lines on the chart is the amount of work remaining. When the project has been completed, the lines will meet.

- The spikes in work scope mean that something has been added to the milestone while spikes in completed work mean a story has been completed. This information can be crucial at retrospective to understand if, for example, too much work has been added or the work has been more complex than estimated.

- Examine the 'Work scope' line to identify any scope creep.

- You can examine the actual and planned start and end dates for each sprint.

Burn down chart

A burndown chart shows the amount of work that has been completed in an epic or sprint, and the total work remaining. Burndown charts are used to predict your team's likelihood of completing their work in the time available. They're also great for keeping the team aware of any scope creep that occurs.

- Click Projects in the navigation bar and select the relevant project

- Click Reports, then select Sprint Burndown Chart.

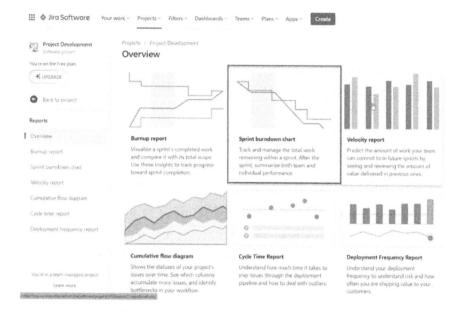

- After that select the sprint and the estimation field. And the chart will be populated.

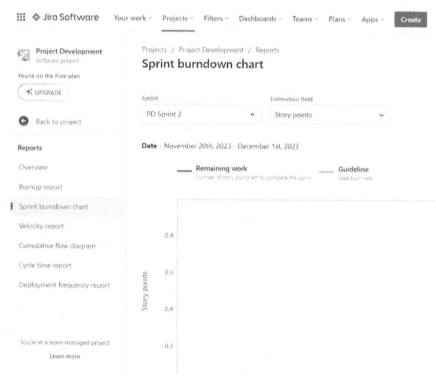

Before you start using the Burndown Chart, you should get to know how it works. The following information will help you understand the key functionalities of the Burndown Chart:

- The Burndown Chart is board-specific – that is, it will only include issues that match your board's saved filter.

- The vertical axis represents the estimation statistic that you have configured for your board.

- The Burndown Chart is based on your board's column mapping. An issue is considered to be 'To Do' when it is in a status that has been mapped to the left-most column of your board. Similarly, an issue is considered to be 'Done' when it is in a status that has been mapped to the right-most column of your board. See Configuring columns for more information.

- If the grey 'Guideline' line does not show, the sprint may have been started before any issues were assigned to it

Velocity, Cycle Time, and Lead Time

Velocity Report

Velocity is the average amount of work a scrum team completes during a sprint. In team-managed Jira Software projects, this can be measured in either story points or number of issues.

Teams can use velocity to predict how quickly they can work through the backlog because the report tracks the forecasted and completed work over several sprints. The more sprints, the more accurate the forecast.

The velocity chart displays the average amount of work a scrum team completes during a sprint. Teams can use velocity to predict how quickly they can work through the backlog because the report tracks the forecasted and completed work over several sprints. The more sprints, the more accurate the forecast.

The chart can be viewed for all Scrum boards and requires that you've completed at least one sprint to show any meaningful data.

To view the Velocity Report, Navigate to your desired board. And Click Reports, then select Velocity Chart.

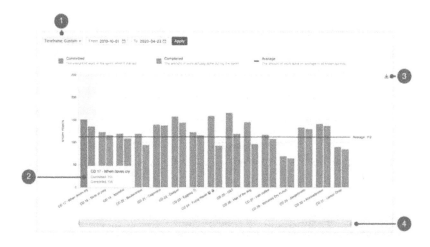

1. **Timeframe**: Choose one of the predefined timeframes, or select a date range. Whatever you choose, it will be retained in the URL, so you can share the link with your teammates.

2. **Sprint details**: Hover over a sprint to see the details, and the work committed and completed. This gives you an idea of whether your team is over- or under-committing. Ideally, the two bars for each sprint should be the same.

3. **Save as image**: Click to save the chart for future reference.

4. **Focus**: Use focus to zoom in on the sprints you're most interested in.

Cycle Time and Lead Time

Jira Cycle time is known as the time it takes for an action to complete from start to finish. It's the phase when the issue is labelled "in progress." The statuses used to compute cycle time are determined by the Jira workflow you're employing.

Jira Lead time refers to the time between receiving a request for an action (not the start of work) and the completion of that action, including time spent in the queue.

The cycle time report helps teams understand how much time it takes to ship issues through the deployment pipeline and how to deal with outliers.

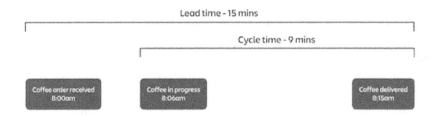

Pre-requisites

- **Connect your source code management and CI/CD tools**

  Your Jira admin needs to have Jira integrated with your CI/CD pipeline. This allows you to receive the deployment data from your connected tools such as Bitbucket Pipelines, GitHub, GitLab, Jenkins, or CircleCI. Learn more about how to use Jira for CI/CD.

- **Make sure you have enough production deployment data**

  To view this report, you need deployment events from your CI/CD tool and commit events from your source code management tool. You must also include issue keys in your branch names, commit messages, and pull requests. Learn how to reference issues in your development work.

- **Check your project and issue-level permissions**

  You need View development tools permission to view the deployment frequency report. Learn more about enabling permissions for your team-managed projects.

To view the cycle time report:

- If not already there, navigate to your Jira Software project.

- From your project's sidebar, select Reports > Overview > Cycle time report.

Agile Metrics and KPIs

Agile metrics provide insight into productivity through the different stages of a software development lifecycle. This helps to assess the quality of a product and track team performance.

Good metrics aren't limited to the reports discussed above. For example, quality is an important metric for agile teams and there are a number of traditional metrics that can be applied to agile development:

- How many defects are found:
  - during development?
  - after release to customers?
  - by people outside of the team?

- How many defects are deferred to a future release?

- How many customer support requests are coming in?

- What is the percentage of automated test coverage?

Agile teams should also look at release frequency and delivery speed. At the end of each sprint, the team should release software out to production. How often is that actually happening? Are most release builds getting shipped? In the same vein, how long does it take for the team to release an emergency fix out to production? Is release easy for the team or does it require heroics?

Agile metrics and kpi's are just one part of building a team's culture. They give quantitative insight into the team's performance and provide measurable goals for the team. While they're important, don't get obsessed. Listening to the team's feedback during retrospectives is equally important in growing trust across the team, quality in the product, and development speed through the release process. Use both quantitative and qualitative feedback to drive change.

Chapter 8
Jira Advanced Topics

Jira Automation

Introduction

Jira Automation is a tool in Jira Software and Jira Cloud that lets people automate their project management tasks by setting up rules. These rules work like 'if this happens, then do that' based on various events in Jira.

It saves time by automating repetitive tasks that usually take up a lot of hours every week. This way, users can concentrate on more important tasks that add value or solve problems.

One cool thing about Jira Automation is that it doesn't require any coding knowledge. Anyone can create these automation rules in Jira, regardless of their technical background.

Key Elements of Automation in Jira

Automation rules are made up of three parts:

- **triggers** that kick off the rule, such as when an issue is created or when a field value is changed.

- **conditions** that refine the rule, For example, you can set up your rule to only escalate an issue if it is high priority.

And lastly

- **actions** that perform tasks in your site, such as editing an issue, sending a notification, or creating sub-tasks.

Notify for high priority issues

(i) **Rule details**
Actor: Jira automation

↳ **When: issue transitioned**
Rule is run when an issue is created.

(•) **If: priority equals**
Highest

(•) **Then: send email**
jira-software-users
{{issue.key}} is of the highest priority!

Add component

How to setup an automation rule in your Jira Project

Navigate to your Jira project board, and then click on the Project settings from the left menu.

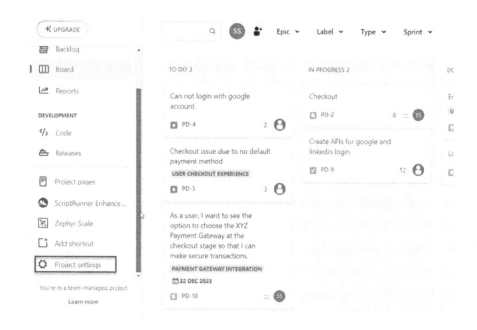

This will redirect you to the project settings, and from there click on the Automation.

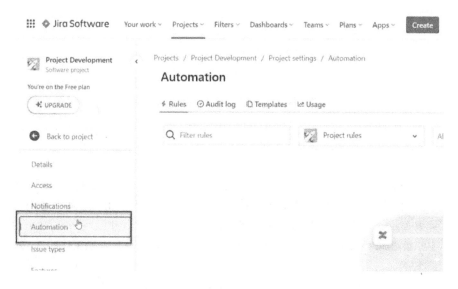

Now click on the Create rule button to create an automation rule. This will open the Rule Builder screen for you.

The first step is to set your trigger. You can select any relevant trigger from the list being shown at the left side. Or you can search for the specific trigger. For now, I am selecting the trigger as "Issue Created"

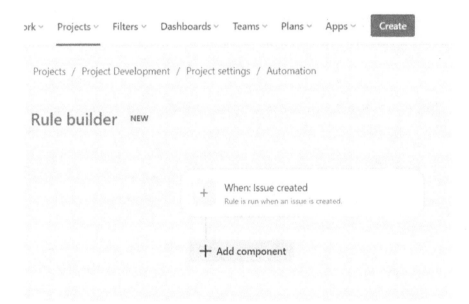

Then the next step is to add a condition. For that, I will click on the "IF: Add a condition" from the left menu, shown in the above screenshot. Here, I am adding a condition, that, if the issue's assignee is empty. So I am selecting the issue fields condition.

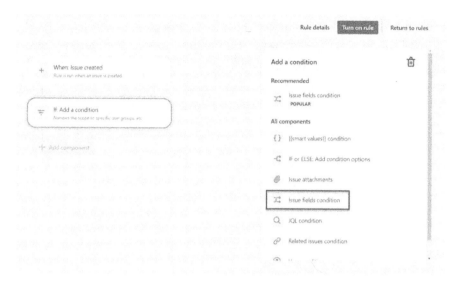

Now in the field, I will select the Assignee field and in the condition I will select "is empty" as a condition. And click next.

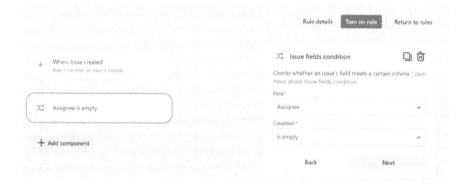

Lastly, I will add the action. So I will click on the Then: Add an action.

Select the Assign issue action and then assign it to the person who must look at the tickets that are unassigned, and get them assigned to the team and get started working on them.

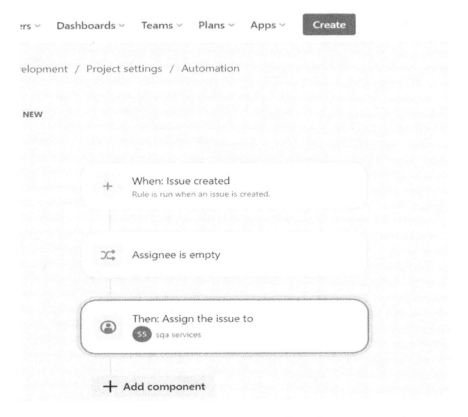

Now that my rule is completed in terms of configuration and setup, I will click on the Turn on rule so that this rule can get started working.

I will name the rule and set the users who can edit the rule.

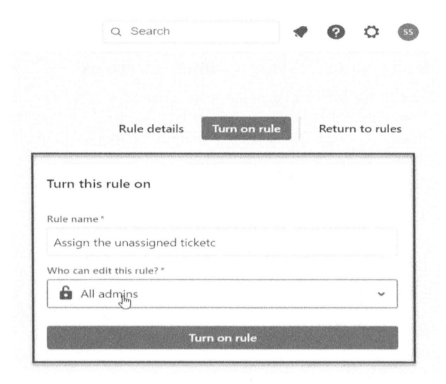

Finally, after doing so, I will click on the Turn on rule to complete the setup.

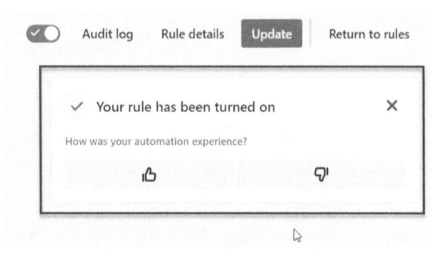

Similarly, you can create many automation rules, as per your project needs and team's efficiency, that will make your project happenings easy.

Enable and disable Jira automation rules

You can view the status of an automation rule to identify if the rule is currently active or not. If a rule is inactive, it will not execute until it is enabled. The status of a rule can be seen on its details screen.

- Enable - The rule is currently active.

- Disable - The rule is not currently in use.

- Draft - The rule has unpublished changes.

When you first create a rule, it is enabled by default.

Disable a rule

To disable a rule, go to the Automation screen or any specific rule and click on the toggle to disable the rule.

Creating new fields in Jira

Custom fields in Jira are user-defined fields that allow you to capture specific information that isn't covered by the default fields provided in Jira. These fields can be tailored to your team or project's unique requirements, enabling you to gather and manage additional data that is important to your workflow.

How to create a custom field?

Click on the gear icon at the top, to open the settings menu. Click on the Issues in the Jira settings.

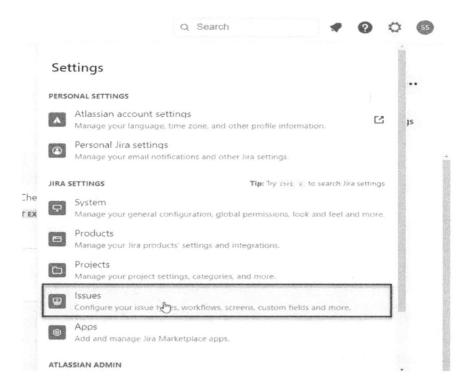

You will see the Fields section in the left menu, and under that, click on the Custom field.

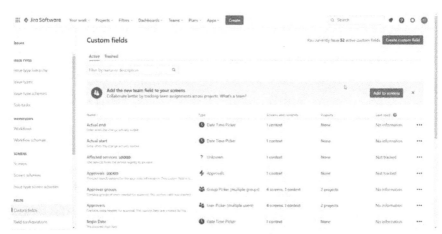

Now click on Create custom field to create a new custom field. You can add any field ranging from checkboxes, drop downs, date time field to creating a plain text field. For now I am creating a plain text field.

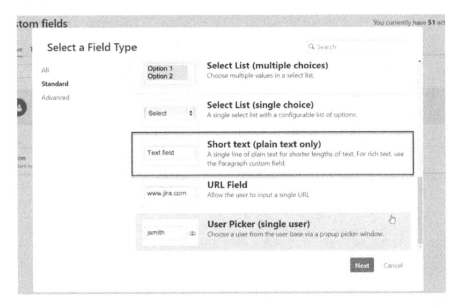

After that, I will give a name to the field and add a description. When I am done with adding this information, I will click on the Create button to add the field.

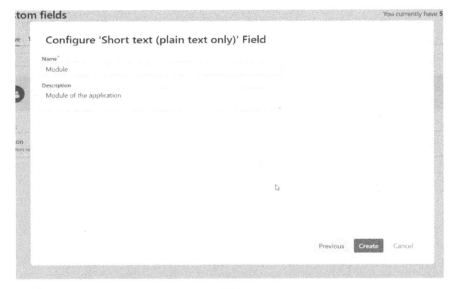

Associate the field with the screen

Once you've made a custom field, you'll be directed to the Screens page. Get additional information about screens from there.

At this point, you can decide where your custom fields should appear on issue screens. For instance, you can opt for them to be visible on screens like the Default screen or Resolve issue screen.

To link the field to these screens, simply check the boxes beside the screens you prefer and then click on the 'Update' button.

The field is now created and associated with the screens.

Display the new field on the issue types screens.

If you have added the new field and have associated with the screens, still if you are not able to view the field on the issue, then you might need to add it on the issue type screen. In order to do that, Go to project settings and then issue types.

Now from the left menu, under the suggested fields, you will be able to see the new field that you created. Drag that up and add it into the custom field on the issue type.

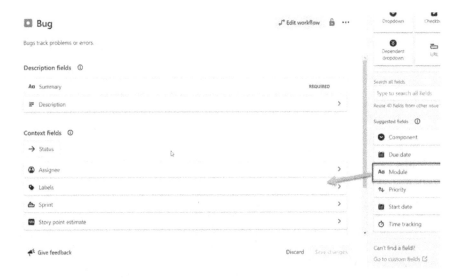

In this way, the field will now show on the issue type when you open it.

Please note that you will need to do this for every issue type in your project, on which you want to display this new field.

Importing Issues/Tasks via CSV

Manually creating large sets of issues in Jira can be time-consuming and error-prone. Importing issues through a CSV file offers a significant advantage in terms of efficiency and accuracy. It allows you to bulk-create in a single action, saving valuable time and reducing the risk of human errors. This method is particularly beneficial for:

- Migrating data from another system to Jira.

- Populating a project with a large backlog of work items.

Preparing you CSV File

- **Structure**: Ensure your CSV file follows a structured format with each row representing a single issue and each column representing a specific Jira field.

- **Headers**: Use clear and concise headers in the first row that correspond to the Jira fields you want to map. Each CSV file must possess a heading row with a summary column and The header row should avoid containing any punctuation (apart from the commas separating each column) or the importer may not work correctly.

- **Field Values:** Choose appropriate values for each field based on Jira's specific format and accepted values. For example, dates should be in the format specified by your Jira instance.

- **Encoding**: Save the file in the correct character encoding (usually UTF-8) to avoid import errors with special characters and Commas (as column/field separators) cannot be omitted

For example, this is valid:

- Summary, Assignee, Reporter, Issue Type, Description, Priority

  "Test issue", bob@example.com, bob@example.com, but this is not valid:

- Summary, Assignee, Reporter, Issue Type, Description, Priority

  "Test issue", bob@example.com, bob@example.com, 1

How to import tasks via CSV

Go to your Jira Project, click on the search bar at the top banner and click on View All issues

At the top right of the page, click on the Three dots, and click on Import issue via CSV.

Now upload your CSV file. And click next.

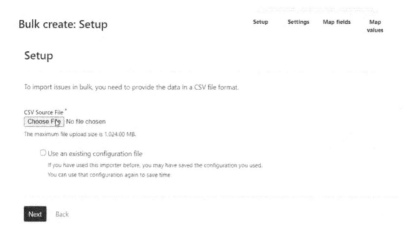

Now select your project in which you want to import the tasks. And keep other settings the same as it is. In case you have made the file in a different way, you may change the values from here.

Settings

Settings

Import to Project *
Select a project   ⌄

File encoding
UTF-8   ⌄

Delimiter *

Please use \t to have a Tabulator character

Date format *
dd/MMM/yy h:mm a

(e.g. dd/MMM/yy h:mm a)
Please specify the format that dates are stored in the CSV file. Please use syntax valid for SimpleDateFormat.

Next   Back

Now, map the CSV fields to the fields in JIRA.

Map fields

Map fields

⚠ Please note: A JIRA **Summary** field mapping is required to enable import.

Select the CSV fields to import, then set how you would like these converted to fields in JIRA. You can optionally map field values on the next screen.

CSV Field	JIRA field	Map field value
Assignee (e.g. First row doesn't have a value)	→ Don't map this field ⌄	
Custom Field 1 (e.g. First row doesn't have a value)	→ Don't map this field ⌄	
Custom Field 2 (e.g. First row doesn't have a value)	→ Don't map this field ⌄	
Description (e.g. This is a test import task)	→ Don't map this field ⌄	
Epic Link (e.g. First row doesn't have a value)	→ Don't map this field ⌄	
Epic Name	→ Don't map this field ⌄	

Once you have mapped all the fields, click next and run the validate function to ensure that everything is fine before the import is initiated.

If there is no issue and you get a success message, you are ready to run the import function. Click on Begin Import and the process will be started.

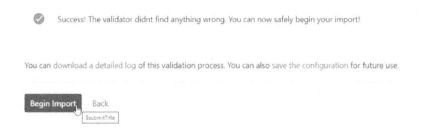

And voila! Your tasks will be imported. Below is the screenshot of the task which I imported.

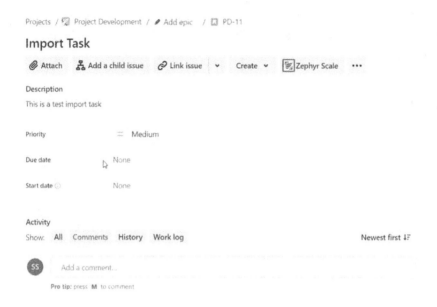

Import Task

Attach   Add a child issue   Link issue   ⌄   Create ⌄   Zephyr Scale   •••

Description

This is a test import task

Priority   Medium

Due date   None

Start date   None

Activity

Show: All   Comments   History   Work log   Newest first ⬇

SS   Add a comment...

Pro tip: press M to comment

Best practices to run Import function in Jira

- Test your CSV file on a small batch of issues before importing a large dataset.

- Ensure you have the necessary permissions to perform import operations.

- Back up your data before any major import procedures.

Bulk Changes/Status Updates

Manually updating numerous issues in Jira can be tedious and time-consuming. Introducing bulk update functionality simplifies processes and enhances team productivity. This built-in Jira feature allows updating multiple issues through a simple interface. You can select issues based on filters, choose fields to update, and define new values. For example, bulk assigning issues to a developer or changing priority across several sprints. Also, you can create complex JQL queries to identify specific issues and execute bulk updates. For instance, updating the sprint field for all open issues due next week.

How to perform Bulk Update

Go to your Jira Project, click on the search bar at the top banner and click on View All issues.

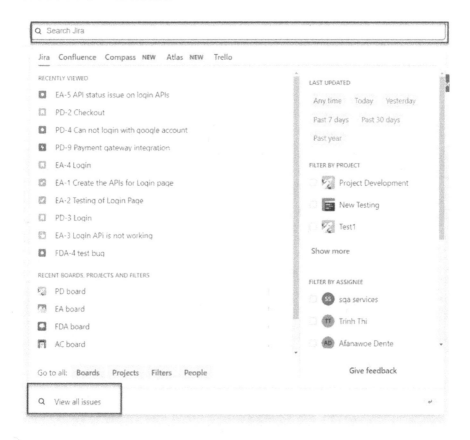

On the View All issue screen, Filter the issues or enter the JQL query to get all the issues you want to update. Once you get a list of all issues, click on the three dots at the top right corner and click on Bulk change all issues

By clicking on it, a new window/tab will be opened, there all your selected issues will be listed, select all of them and click on Next button.

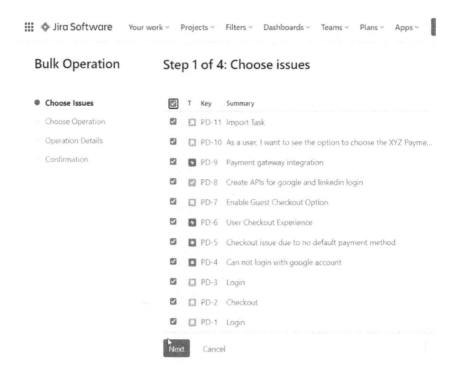

On the next step, choose the action you want to perform on the selected issues. All the possible actions you can perform are listed here.

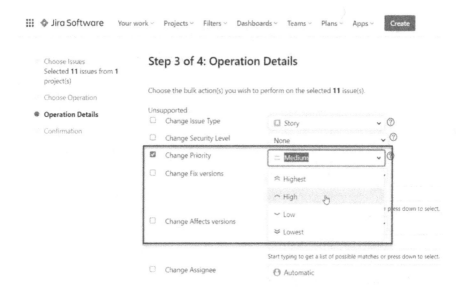

Step 2 of 4: Choose bulk action

Choose which action you'd like to take on the selected issues.

Learn more about each bulk action

○ Edit Issues	Edit field values of issues
○ Move Issues	Move issues to new projects and issue types
○ Transition Issues	Transition issues through workflow
○ Delete Issues	Permanently delete issues from Jira
○ Watch Issues	Watch all the selected issues. You will receive notifications when any of these issues are updated.
○ Stop Watching Issues	Stop watching all the selected issues. You will no longer receive notifications when any of these issues are updated.

Next   Cancel

For now, I am using the Edit Issues option and after that click on Next. On the next step, I will select the field which needs to be updated in bulk on all the selected tickets. For example, if I need to change the priority of all the selected from Medium to High, I will select the High from the drop down in the priority field. And click Next.

⚏ ◆ Jira Software   Your work ˅   Projects ˅   Filters ˅   Dashboards ˅   Teams ˅   Plans ˅   Apps ˅   Create

Choose Issues
Selected 11 issues from 1
project(s)

Choose Operation

● Operation Details

Confirmation

Step 3 of 4: Operation Details

Choose the bulk action(s) you wish to perform on the selected 11 issue(s).

Unsupported

☐ Change Issue Type   🗔 Story   ˅ ⓘ

☐ Change Security Level   None   ˅ ⓘ

☑ Change Priority   ☰ Medium   ˅ ⓘ

☐ Change Fix versions   ⌃ Highest

                              ⌃ High   🖑

☐ Change Affects versions   ˅ Low   r press down to select.

                              ≫ Lowest

                              Start typing to get a list of possible matches or press down to select.

☐ Change Assignee   ⊖ Automatic

183

I will confirm the changes on the next screen, and click on the Confirm button to finally initiate the bulk update function.

Click on the Acknowledge button, once the bulk function is run successfully.

Bulk Operation

Bulk Operation Progress

Editing 11 issues

Bulk operation is 100% complete.
Task completed in 1 second
Started Today 11:31 PM.
Finished Today 11:31 PM.

Acknowledge

Jira Notifications and Alerts

Jira Software Notifications and Alerts are powerful tools to keep users informed about important activity within projects. Notifications are automated messages sent via email or other channels when specific events occur (e.g. issue created, comment added, status changed).

How to set up project related notifications

Go to your project > 'Settings' > 'Issues' > 'Notification Schemes.'

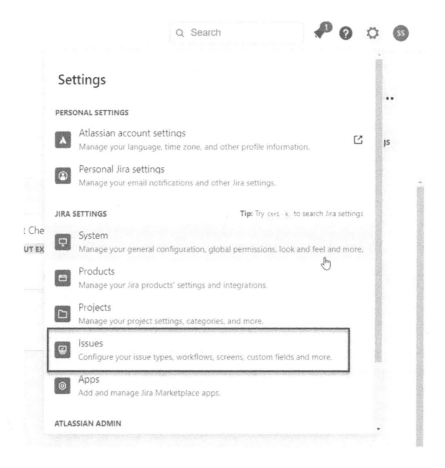

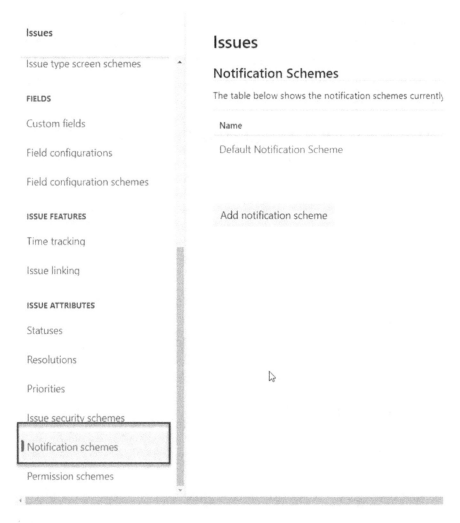

Edit or create notification schemes linked to specific projects. Click on Notifications in the Action column to edit the notifications.

You can view all the notifications set up in this screen, and if you want to set up the new notification alert on any event, click on Add new notification.

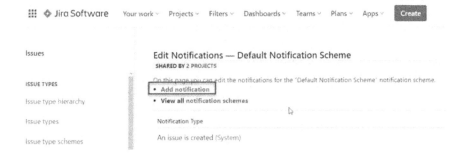

Select the notification type from a list, where all the events are listed like An issue is created or someone made a comment and after that select the user/group which would receive the notification.

Once you are done, click on Add, and the new notification will be created in the system.

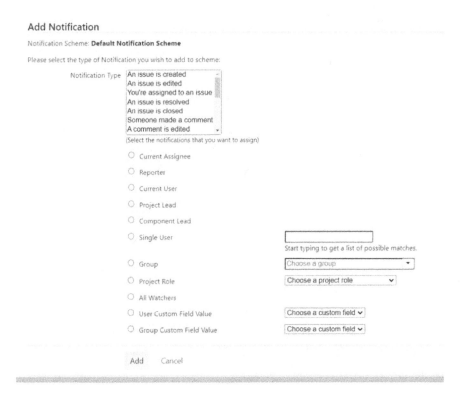

Similarly, you can delete the recipients from the notifications, if required or needed.

Turning on/off email notifications

When the notifications are configured, you also receive the email alerts for the notifications. You can turn on/off and limit the email alerts for the notifications. For that, click on the settings or the gear icon at the top bar, and go to personal settings.

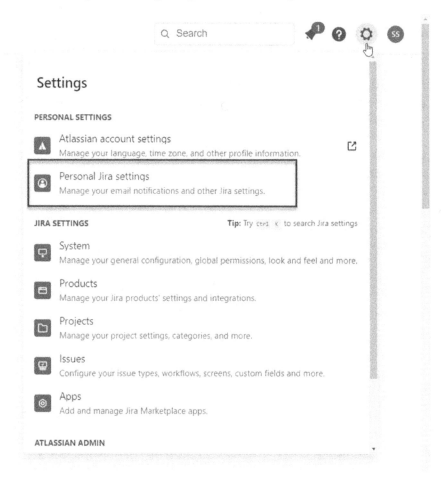

Under that, You will see a section where the Email notifications configurations are available. You can make changes as per your requirements and click on done. By default, there are some configurations set up already.

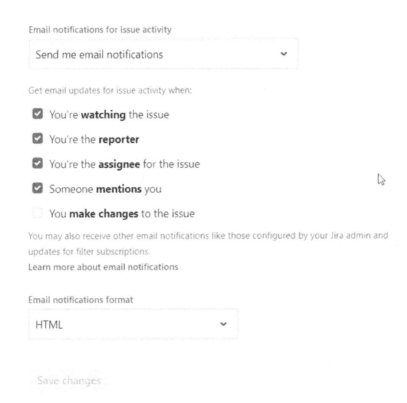

Email notifications for issue activity

Send me email notifications ⌄

Get email updates for issue activity when:

✅ You're **watching** the issue

✅ You're the **reporter**

✅ You're the **assignee** for the issue

✅ Someone **mentions** you

☐ You **make changes** to the issue

You may also receive other email notifications like those configured by your Jira admin and updates for filter subscriptions.

Learn more about email notifications

Email notifications format

HTML ⌄

Save changes

Jira Plugin/Add-Ons

Jira boasts the capability to enhance its functionality through the installation of add-ons or plugins. An add-on is an installable component that complements or extends the features of Jira. For instance, the Jira Calendar Plugin is an add-on that presents due dates for issues and versions in a calendar format. Additional add-ons facilitate connections between Jira and Bamboo, aid in Jira development, and enable seamless access to Atlassian support directly from the Jira platform.

Jira is equipped with pre-installed add-ons known as system apps. However, users have the flexibility to expand the functionality further by installing additional add-ons. This can be achieved either by obtaining an add-on from the Atlassian Marketplace or by uploading an add-on directly from the local file system. Remarkably, users can even install add-ons they have developed themselves, providing a high level of customization.

To install the addons from the marketplace, navigate to Apps section and click on explore more apps.

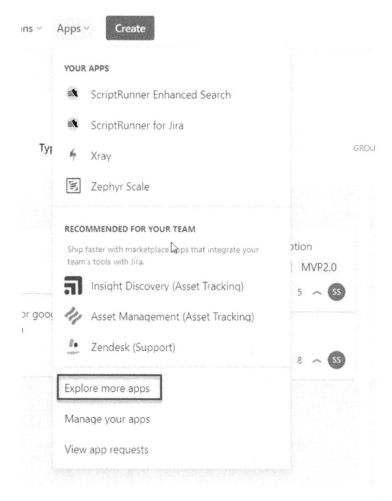

This will lead you to the Marketplace, from where you can search and install apps.

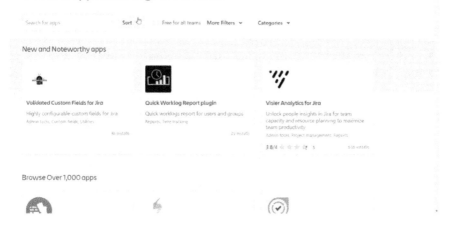

And when you want to add any marketplace app in your jira, just click on the Add button and the app will be installed on your Jira.

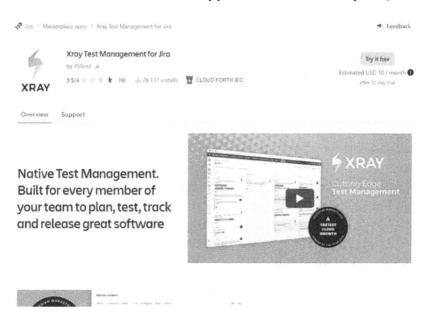

Glossary

- **Agile**: A methodology that promotes continuous iteration of development and testing throughout the project lifecycle.

- **Backlog**: A prioritized list of tasks or features to be worked on, maintained by the product owner.

- **Burndown Chart**: A graphical representation of the amount of work remaining versus time, used in Scrum to track sprint progress.

- **Capacity Planning**: The process of determining the amount of work a team can commit to in a sprint based on past performance and available resources.

- **Dashboard**: A customizable workspace in Jira that displays project data, such as charts or lists, providing real-time project insights.

- **Dependency**: A relationship between two issues where one depends on the completion of the other.

- **Epic**: A large user story or feature that can be broken down into smaller tasks or stories.

- **Estimation**: The process of predicting the amount of effort or time required to complete a task or story, often measured in story points or time.

- **Filter**: A saved search in Jira used to quickly find issues that match specified criteria.

- **Issue**: A generic term for any task, bug, story, or subtask that represents work to be done in Jira.

- **Issue Linking**: The process of connecting related issues in Jira to show dependencies or relationships.

- **Jira Query Language (JQL)**: A powerful query language used to search for issues in Jira based on custom criteria.

- **Kanban**: A visual framework used to implement Agile that helps teams visualize their work and optimize flow.

- **Kanban Board**: A tool used to manage work in progress by visualizing it as cards on a board with columns that represent different stages of work.

- **Label**: A tag or keyword used to categorize issues in Jira for easier tracking and filtering.

- **Release**: A set of features or tasks that are completed and delivered as part of a product update or deployment.

- **Scrum**: An Agile framework that uses sprints, time-boxed iterations of work, to organize tasks and deliver value incrementally.

- **Scrum Board**: A visual representation of tasks and their status during a sprint, used in Scrum methodology.

- **Sprint**: A set period during which specific work from the backlog is completed and made ready for review.

- **Sprint Backlog**: A subset of the product backlog consisting of tasks selected for completion in a sprint.

- **Story Points**: A unit of measure for estimating the relative effort of a task or story in Agile.

- **Subtask**: A smaller piece of work within a larger parent issue, breaking down more complex tasks into manageable parts.

- **Swimlane**: A horizontal row in a Kanban or Scrum board used to categorize issues by different criteria, such as priority or team member.

- **Task**: A small, individual piece of work that contributes to completing a user story or project.

- **Test-Driven Development (TDD)**: A software development practice where tests are written before the code to guide development and ensure high-quality output.

- **Time Tracking**: A Jira feature that allows users to log time spent on tasks, useful for monitoring progress and workload.

- **Transition**: The process of moving an issue from one status to another in Jira workflows.

- **User Role**: A specific set of permissions or capabilities assigned to a user in Jira, such as Administrator, Member, or Viewer.

- **User Story**: A description of a feature or functionality written from the perspective of the end user, representing a unit of work.

- **Velocity**: The amount of work a team completes during a sprint, used as a measure of team performance and capacity planning.

- **WIP (Work in Progress) Limits**: Constraints set on the number of tasks allowed in a given stage to ensure that team members aren't overloaded.

- **Workflow**: A predefined sequence of steps that an issue follows from creation to completion in Jira.

- **Worklog**: A record of time logged against an issue, showing the time spent and the progress made.

- **Burndown Velocity**: A metric used to track the rate at which the team is completing work in a sprint, visualized through a burndown chart.

- **Automation Rule**: A rule in Jira that allows automatic actions, such as sending notifications or updating issue statuses, based on triggers or conditions.

- **Sprint Goal**: The overarching objective of a sprint that provides focus and helps the team measure success at the end of the iteration.

- **Jira Permissions**: Settings that define what actions users can perform in a project, such as creating, editing, or deleting issues.

- **Custom Field**: A user-defined field in Jira that can be added to an issue to capture specific information not covered by standard fields.

- **Epic Link**: A connection between a user story and the epic it belongs to, used to track progress toward larger goals.

- **Resolution**: The final status or outcome of an issue, such as "Done," "Won't Fix," or "Duplicate."

About the Author

Bringing over 17 years of leadership experience, Dr Francis Mbunya is an accomplished Executive Coach and Agile Product Delivery Expert & Trainer, specializing in guiding enterprise agile transformations. As a seasoned subject matter expert, his proficiency spans diverse areas such as agile transformation facilitation, change management, conflict resolution, stakeholder engagement, product roadmap creation, release planning, design thinking, and maturity assessments. Dr. Francis practical expertise extends to various agile project management tools, including Agile View, Agile Plan, Jira, Jira Align, Service Now, PowerBI, Rally, and Azure DevOps. By applying agile principles, he excels in developing and facilitating business value delivery, aligning strategic goals with budget constraints, and establishing high-performing agile product delivery teams. Recognized for his exceptional communication, leadership, interpersonal, and business analytical skills, he is confident in his ability to make a significant contribution to your team.

www.ingramcontent.com/pod-product-compliance
Lightning Source LLC
LaVergne TN
LVHW051230050326
832903LV00028B/2323